Emily Thacher B Bennett

Song of the Rivers

Emily Thacher B Bennett

Song of the Rivers

ISBN/EAN: 9783743303669

Manufactured in Europe, USA, Canada, Australia, Japa

Cover: Foto ©Thomas Meinert / pixelio.de

Manufactured and distributed by brebook publishing software (www.brebook.com)

Emily Thacher B Bennett

Song of the Rivers

Song of the Rivers.

BY

EMILY T. B. BENNETT.

The beings of the mind are not of clay;
Essentially immortal, they create
And multiply in us a brighter ray
And more beloved existence: that which Fate
Prohibits to dull life, in this our state
Of mortal bondage.   *   *   *—CHILDE HAROLD.

From earth's bright faces fades the light of morn,
From earth's glad voices drops the joyous tone;
But ye, the children of the soul, were born
Deathless, and for un lying love alone:
And O! ye beautiful! 'tis well, how well,
In the soul's world with you, where change is not, to dwell!—HEMANS.

DEDICATORY.

To every heart in my now eminently free native land; gratefully including those dear friends whose spontaneous sympathy and partial judgment have proven my surest source of inspiration; with far less less of the noble, arbitrary power of art, than the simple, warm impulse of nature, do I pleasurably and trustingly inscribe these imperfect perceptions of life's philosophy and poetry, only asking of those who may generously give them their brief attention, the exercise of sweet charity and the kindness of universal love.

E. T. B. B.

CINCINNATI, 1865.

CONTENTS.

After the press work of this poem had commenced, a fire occurred in
the stereotyping rooms, leaving a number of the plates in a damaged
condition, which were hastily re-set and re-cast, but not without the
following

ERRATA :

Page 84, 7th line is omitted: read

"Then from the viney alcove he withdrew."

85, 4th line, for "flowers" read "flours."
97, 1st line, for "brambling" read "branding."
100, 5th line, for "bower" read "bowed."
100, 22d line, for "up" read "upon."
121, 24th line, for "explorer's" read "explorers."
166, Last line, read "As mild as Cautantowit's breath bestows."
184, 7th line, for "raptuous" read "raptnrous."
218, 5th line, for "heart" read "harp."
244, Last line is omitted : read "The queen of all its floral train."

CONTENTS.

SONG OF THE RIVERS.

SONG OF THE RIVERS.

Mild Genoa whose sunny slope
   First met our 'Sea-king's' eyes
Deep in immeasurable hope,
   And slumbrous destinies,—
Home of our land's discoverer,
We greet thee from its templed shore !

Columbus, star of time, 'tis thee—
   God's true interpreter
Of science and immensity,—
   Most royal mariner
Of mountain waves, thy secret keeping,—
Thee pride salutes, the past o'ersweeping !

Sea-winds moved gently on that day,
   Hushed Tritons swam below,
Awed by the new persuasive ray
   That lit the Old World's brow,
Illuminating History's shroud,
Extending Ocean's outlines broad .

Spain fed the fire of that young soul,—
 A queen bestowed her smile ;—
Launched—onward to the goal,
 To continent or isle,
Bidding Futurity, 'all hail,'
Those heroes of the tide set sail.

Glory allures with phantom arms
 Man's soul to her embrace ;
While he pursues, recede her charms,
 Still dazzling, giving place
To empty air, or scorpion stings,
When feels the mind bereft of wings.

Say, was it this that lured them on,—
 Adventurers so bold;
Till when long lonely months were gone
 Calm trust relaxed its hold
On men unnerved by shoreless seas,
Their leader's voice could scarce appease?

Glory and gain—by these possest,
 Love mingling some faint hue;
When danger weakened each strong breast,
 Doubting if Heaven were true,
Denied hope's anchor, tossed and broken,
Reproach became their spirit's token.

But he, the king of that sail realm,
 Wilt call him else than brave

While watching o'er his vessel's helm
The flashing of the wave,—
Deny we him true glory's smile,
Or ask if there he sighed the while?

No! no! a stronger soul was his,
Prophetic in its fire,
Life's benefaction crowning bliss,
Which deepening, pointing higher,
Defined far o'er the sea's fair shores
Waiting to greet The Nations' oars.

'A light! a light!' An island lone
Adds lustre to the stars!
And, in the misty morning's dawn
'Land!' breaks the watery bars:—
'SAN SALVADOR,' an islet gem
Transferred to Castile's diadem!

Years pass: again and yet again
A continent was sought—
Ah! who asserts, in vain, in vain
Columbus nursed the thought
Which gave his name to realms like these
Bounding the poles and sovereign seas!

The Western World a myth no more,
The hero wanderer died;
Where rest his bones, that land and shore
May cherish them in pride;—

A life-time dream became its trust,
And honored sleeps Italian dust.

While centuries their courses rolled
    Ambition lured its slaves,
Who sought distinction, fame and gold,
    And found — ignoble graves,—
Contentment's treasures, sorrow's cost,
By thought's infatuation lost.

De Leon for this new-found sphere
    Embarked with trusting dreams,
Seeking a fount whose ripples clear,
    And pure immortal gleams,
Could check the beautiful's decay
And make youth's morn an endless May.

He found a land of wondrous bloom,
    Where trees were gay with flowers,
Where many a sylvan streamlet's tune
    Courted the lingering hours,
Where rich luxuriant Nature shone
In solitude, but not alone.

Bird, insect, beast and waterfall
    Blended their music there;
Great Nature swelling at their call
    Woke zephyrs from the air,
Nor need had she for man to sing
Response to her perpetual Spring.

But for man's soul no wave was found
    With youth's elixir fraught;
Death whispered still, 'by me ye're bound,—
    I scorn your deathless thought;
Eden is here, but sin is thine,—
The curse of toil and age is mine.'

FERNANDO SOTO caught the fire
    Of wild ambition's aim,
Intrepid in his soul's desire,
    Dazzled by hopes of fame
He sped impetuous o'er the way,
    His motto 'Spain and Florida.'

Upon the new, bewildering strand
    His followers watched his eye;
Raising aloft his graceful hand,
    He spoke, '*success or die!*'
Then o'er the flowery plains untried
They marched with danger for their guide.

Not spectres of the dismal swamp,
    Nor prowling Indian's hate,
Nor panthers howling round their camp
    Revoked their wandering fate;
While threading wild or fording wave
Unfaltering long their hearts were brave.

Thus summers passed;—mild winters wore
    With march and death away;

Scarce came brief tidings from the shore
   Of Spain or Florida ;—
When fears were spoken, Soto frowned,—
His 'El Dorado' still unfound.

Leaving blue Alabama's tide,
   Their numbers growing less,
The remnant marched with gloomy stride
   West in the wilderness ;
They thought not how their mission's power
Outran the years, to *this* grand hour !

Lo ! bursting on their weary gaze
   A mighty stream is flowing
Beneath the forest's tangled maze,
   With sunset changes glowing :
Slowly it rolls—an endless sea,
Majestic, deep, perpetually.

Three hundred buried years have told
   Time's stories of the past ;
Of all its pages free from mould
   One record shines forecast,
So long as Mississippi flows
To tropic seas from Arctic snows.

The Bow of Commerce spans in pride
   From bank to bank its wave
And never bends but where the tide
   Sweeps o'er De Soto's grave :

Breaking the shade of chambers deep,
Its hues grow brighter o'er his sleep.

Meanwhile unnumbered cycles gray
   May wreathe the shaft of time,
Illumined till the latest day
   To make his fate sublime,
A shadow and a radiance mild,
Tablet for one adventurous child.

   *   *   *   *   *   *

Behold the wasting of a dream,
   While flickers life's spent lamp !
The tents are pitched beside the stream,
   Low murmurs from the camp
Whisper that now the hand of death
   Is slowly stealing Soto's breath.

An Indian maiden fans his brow,
   Her coal-tinged eyes are deep ;
Her tears as when the south-winds blow
   Rain as the blossoms weep,
Falling upon the sufferer's cheek
   Whose eye of pride is strangely meek.

And by his couch a Spaniard stands,
   Accepting hope's despair ;
Bending to clasp his leader's hands
   He something whispers there

Which life's vague wandering gaze enchains,
Brightening mid death's all-conquering pains.

He speaks:— 'Moscoso! no return
    Shall let me conquer more;
Ambition's fires have ceased to burn,—
    Farewell, my native shore,—
To mortal man I never bowed,
But now I kiss Jehovah's rod.

'In my own river, folded round
    With Castile's banner wide,—
In midnight's silent hour profound,
    Entomb me in its tide:
Consign me to my wave-walled home
With lighted torch and roll of drum.

'Unpaled by man, unknown to fear,
    Alone, O let me sleep:
The conqueror—discoverer,
    Desires no eye to weep
His watery grave so early made
Far west of Florid's everglade.

'Moscoso, hear, my follower brave,
    My dying words obey;
Cross not the wilderness; the wave
    More safely shall convey
The remnant of my people back
From this illusive, dangerous track.'

He from his withered hand withdrew
  An ancient massive ring,
And while his lips more livid grew,
  And fainter ebbed life's spring,
Moscoso reverently wore
  The pledge his master's finger bore.

Now noiseless through the tent
  A savage warrior strides ;
His plume is by the curtain bent,
  The wampum girds his sides ;
His lineaments with war-paint black,
And shades of death are in his track !

A Natchez chief to challenge war ;
  His tawny neck arrayed
In chains of cougar's claws, and hair
  Of human tresses made :
One hand contains a war-pipe red,
Its mate an emblem ever dread—

A bunch of poisoned arrows bound
  With skin of rattlesnake ;
He broke a silence deep, profound
  As midnight o'er a lake,
While on the couch the gift he flung,
The war-whoop rising from his tongue.

Symbols that spoke the deadly hate
  Of this most warlike tribe

Who save by these gave no debate,
 Received nor price nor bribe,—
Pursuing with revengeful breath
The white chief to his verge of death.

Defiantly he raised the pipe,—
 No calumet of peace,—
The stern, complete, embodied type
 Of a relentless race;
Its rising smoke but slowly curled,
 For Soto lingered in the world.

The leader watched the potent scene,
 With one unearthly moan—
But angered, unrelenting mien,
 His arms were upward thrown;
He clutched the covering of his bed
As though 'twere lance or rapier dread.

With one fierce bound he forward sprang
 His features flashing fire;
'St Jago!' 'Spain,' 'De Soto,' rang
 In stern victorious ire,
Then death the struggle made complete,—
He fell beside the Indian's feet.

Ambition! Ruler of the soul!
 When monarch there thou art,
To many a strange uncertain goal
 Thou leadest mind and heart—

Thou wild inspirer of the breast
That ever after feels no rest!

The sun had set o'er wave and wild;
  The noon of darkness breathed
Life-tainting damps; bright stars were piled
  High up the dome, and wreathed
The ebon brow of night, that bade
Its silence chill o'er bluff and glade.

Five hundred torches flaming red
  Illumed a funeral track,
While holy priest with censor led
  The train o'er waters black,
And high *Te Deum* anthems gave
Solemnity to air and wave.

With Castile's ensign gaily bound,
  Still upright as in life,
With sword in hand, by helmet crowned,—
  All powerless for strife,—
The dark canoe with silent oar
His corse o'er turbid waters bore

Grim shades commingling with the gleam
  Sent awe to every man;
Midway the dark sepulchral stream
  A signal from the van
Sank in the flow each lurid light,
And all was dark as Stygian night.

As down the lifeless burden fell
  No noisy plunge was heard;
O'er rippling wave or distant dell
  Went forth no echoing word,
And slowly turned each fragile bark
To follow shade or meteor spark.

At dawn the wild beasts roaming near
  Broke forth their sullen roar,
And Indians in their coverts drear
  Felt Soto was—no more;
Still moved the Mississippi on,
As calmly as through ages gone.

———

Land of the pilgrim's love! New England green!
Above thy hills the brightest skies are seen;
Around thy groves and spires swell purest airs,—
Thy bosom nature's noblest children bears!
Thy vine-wreathed homes and monuments of mind,
Fondly in memory's urn are all enshrined

Fair stream! the pride of my own native glen,
Bright line of olden heraldry, again
My feet would press thy bank serene,
Thou circling radiance! thou river queen!
Mild Housatonic! thy eccentric tide
Circles the valley of my father's pride;

And when my eye surveys thy graceful sweep,
E'en for the sorrows of his youth I weep.
Still 'neath thy elm tree shades, with ceaseless tone
Sighing thy requiems for heroes gone,
Perpetuate the sympathetic strains
When nevermore the red man roves thy plains ;
But let the music of the cultured soul
Thy most enduring harmonies control !
Where wild Missouri's dusky flood maintains
Its wavering course through groves and bluff-bound
     plains,
The remnant of a wandering tribe* supply
The hunting grounds thy fertile fields deny;
Named by their dark forefathers, thou
A seal baptismal bearest on thy brow,
Which changing ages never shall efface,
Though lost in sands, forgotten be thy place !

Now by a mightier river's curving side
I stand and watch its majesty of tide,
Asking in vain of some remoter morn
When for this path its sovereignty was born !
'Tis solitude around me ; I but hear
With spirit sense, an angel whisperer,
Invoking memory to write the tale
Which once from fading lips, and frail,
Revealed to me,—a stranger wandering here—
The story of a dying one, with smile and tear

*The Stockbridge tribe.

So sweet, so limpid, each became the seal
Of all truth's inspiration might reveal.
And, reader, turn with me thy pensive gaze
Toward this summer sun's retreating rays—
Behold a narrow mound o'ershadowed by
The neighboring forests sentry, broad and high,
A balsam pine, which mournful, mournful sings,
With every tune each wind and season brings.
I stand beside thee, but in thought away,
Through blooming fields and shaded dells I stray,
Sail o'er bright waters, thread dark forests through,
O'er mountain summits fringed with heaven's blue,
Till 'mong the hills and vales again I stand,
Beside the river of my fatherland :
On Housatonic's bank,—my fingers weave
Of willows green, a wreath for yonder grave ;
In memory's sweet refrain which love bestows,
I pluck the treasures of the wayside rose,
Mingling some everlasting buds, I seek
To make the crown a heavenly story, speak ;—
Memorial—fair trophy of the East.
I'd lay it where our wanderer's relics rest.

'Twas May—a morning bright, and years ago,—
Serenely mild and blue, the river's flow
Circled a happy vale by mountains crowned,
An emerald gem by graceful distance bound ;
Violets starred with blue its meadow grass
Whose cowslips scarce would let the sunbeams pass :

There flowed a brook's perpetual, laughing tide,
Whose spray shed burnished diamonds far and wide,
Moistening the wanton lambkin's snowy fleece,
Bidding the spotted lily bloom in peace ;—
And there a white and humble cottage stood,
With oaken floors, and windows low and rude,
Beloved by many a tendril of the vine,
Whose shades spoke early of the sun's decline.
On that fair morn, a sweet May flower unrolled
Its outer petals, roseate to behold,
But not to wither like the rose of Spring,
Not fleeting as the red-bird's coral wing
This infant girl on youthful parents smiled,
An early hope, a consecrated child ;
Another self to guide in wisdom's ways,
A soul to tune for Heaven's immortal lays.
Like rills unprisoned, dancing, bright and strong,
Anticipations woke with hope and song
Of joys that led the future's angel train,
Bringing sweet antidotes for transient pain.

The child of wedded love, love was her **air,**
Her earliest food ;—so gentle and so fair
Was she ! Affection never clung
To stronger hearts like viney tendrils hung
In oak tree bowers : her eyes, full, large and blue.
Mimosa-like, from look severe withdrew :
Her presence then and ever, was akin
To joy that spirits feel unknown to sin ;

But Earth ne'er offers bliss so full, the draught
Commingles no illusive drops when quaffed.

She grew, a duteous and an only child,
From year to year with richer promise smiled;
No brother roved with her in sprightly mien
The wildwood shades, and sunny pastures green;
No sister's hand of blossoms white and rare
Wove crowns to bind her curling auburn hair,
Yet she was happy, artless, pure and free,
A flower, a singing bird, a honey bee.
She learned the homes of all the vernal flowers,
And sought their smiles in these warm freshening hours
That follow winter's chill receding reign,
Ere yet young grasses clothe the ground again.
The small wind flower* whose robe no color cost,
Displayed a central star with petals lost;
Ephemeral, its fragile being told
Of joyless hearts, when love has left them cold.
Polygalas† of purple crest displayed
Their royal bloom in wood and leaf-strewn glade,
When shone their fringy eyes up through the tomb
Of last year's verdure — proof of autumn's gloom.
When June advanced with gorgeous robes and sheen,
And Earth re-smiled in garniture of green,
The wild rose on the hill its blossoms gave,
And hawthorn clusters, white as foaming wave;
Allien made these her toys, while fancies sweet

*Anemone nemorosa.   † Polygala paucifolia.

Assumed the hue of petals at her feet,
Bright as the fragrant coronets she wove
For her whom nature taught a daughter's love.
Of leaves — her childhood's laurels — too, she twined
Garlands of play her father's hat to bind,
Richer to him than fame's or victor's crown,—
The love of his sweet girl was all his own.
She was a friend to every breathing thing :
The tiniest life, the bird of smallest wing,
The humming insect,— e'en the reptile's form
Her kind, indulgent heart wonld weep to harm ;—
And thus she lived, and grew, a thoughtful girl,
With step of grace, and lip of beauty's curl,
And love-deep dreaming eye.

An ideal sense
Of something faultless, Eden's fair defense,
A creature formed for love, for grief,— for sin,—
Is woman frail and changing ; yet within
Her ofttimes contradicted soul may rest.
Strong faculties that wait some future test
Storms with one stroke rend oaks in centuries grown,
One shock, and all their gathered strength is gone !
So man may fall, and want the envied power
Gently possessed by one elastic flower.

Who knows how girlhood learns by heart its dreams,
How fancy then paints such bewitching scenes
Whose clouds are silken curtains, hiding more
Than they reveal — whose faults we scarce deplore ;

Who knows on what a bright shore its footsteps
    stand,
Looking afar, as toward its native land,
For joys unnamed, untasted, undefined,—
Love's gentle angels of the unscathed mind?

The life of young Allien now more mature,
Love's sweet mysterious desires allure
The pure affection of the infant heart
To fuller, warmer, more impassioned art:
Vaguely she estimated, but she knew
Something there was unknown to her, so true
Of heart delight, that once to feel its thrill,
Was ecstacy's enslavement of the will

The fair love-calling of her sixteenth Spring
Causes her soul from deeper founts to sing,
And life is paradise in vistas green
Whose glimpses come etherial folds between.
When sunset tells the recreative hour,
And richer odors wander from the flower,
More oft she seeks her favorite chosen bower;—
'Tis now her mother's heart begins to miss
Her long companionship and frequent kiss,
Forgetting, as alas! we all forget
That once the youth whose exile we regret
Was but a tissue of romantic dreams,
Of glowing thoughts and joy bewildering schemes;
Of sympathies that sought their genial home

In hearts as young as ours ; when we would roam
In soft imagination's tropic bowers,
And crown the brow we loved with orange flowers

Meanwhile there came from a far distant land
Letters, long intervals between ;—one hand,
Obeying one true heart ne'er failed its token,—
Its strong fraternal pledge remained unbroken,
And from the Manor's cheery ingle-side
A brother's love flew o'er the sea in pride :—
Allien would listen while these pages read
Told the brief story that some friend was dead ;
Or wedding tales ;—of children born, or cares
That strengthened like the wheat-besetting tares ;
Or e'en perchance how some brave highland clan
In battle pitched, unwavered in the van :
And last,—disheartening hope—that still the sire,
Trembling with age had ne'er revoked his ire.
She listened and she sighed as memory's jewels fell,—
Wept with her mother, why she could not tell :
Why kindle now her soft expectant een
To brighter flash each silken fringe between,
While laughter curls her pretty lip with joy
Through tidings of a distant cousin-boy ?

Young Agnes Ramsey, daughter of the swain,
Was loved by Robert, heir of proud Glenwayne ;
Her brow and lip—a lily and a rose ;—
Her simple truth, the richest dower he chose.

Braving his father's fierce relentless pride,
Agnes became his chosen, honored bride ;
And exiled thus, they found a foreign home,
From whence they sought no more o'er Earth to roam.
A fair New-England valley thus became
Their rest ; Glendale they called its simple name,
But never should it know the *pibroch's* sound
On the hoarse bag-pipe's ancient mountain round ;
Ne'er tremble 'neath the war-clan's treading shock,
When bugle blasts re-echo from the rock,
In signal for each hardy mountaineer
Among the chieftain's gathering to appear.
And these the parents of the fair Allien,
In solitude some happiness had seen,
Albeit the vigor and the power of thought
Which but with man's more active life is brought,
Denied, their simple lives at least were pure,
Needing for misanthropic hearts no cure.

Young Oscar was an heir of lordly state,
Of halls long honored by the lineal great,
Around which aged parks, and velvet lawns
Swept far and near ; where deer and spotted fawns
Gamboled in freedom ; where exotics bloomed
In vast conservatories ;—palm-trees plumed
With rain-bows—children of a gorgeous clime,—
The crimson cactus, orange sweet, and lime ;
Mimosas from Brazil, whose veins
Recoiled as though the human touch brought stains ;

Callas from Ethiopia's ardent river,—
White sheaths of maiden bloom unstained, and ever ;
And fern-acacias sweetening all the air
Which softly slumbers in their emerald hair :
And there, in hours of study and of play,
Oscar sends winged, roving thoughts away,
Vainly imploring fancy to present
His cousin's face to charm his discontent ;
Mirage of childhood, ere youth's glow began,—
Ere dignity upon his brow wrote 'MAN.'
O, such young years are purple clouds at dawn,
Dispelling while the vision rests thereon ;
Which life's meridian says are dreams of dreams,
Mist-vails that glitter o'er uncertain streams !
The iris, beauty's most transporting form,
Not merely bounds the archway of the storm,
But oft a dual glory it displays,
One bow so bright it duplicates its rays ;
Thus childhood glows, and youth, though more serene,
Spans, like a rainbow reproduced, life's scene.

Oscar would see Columbia's famous shore,
Whose story time sings grandly, o'er and o'er ;
The empire child of Briton's regime old,
Whose sons for freedom's promise grew so bold.
And he would meet his father's distant friends,
Perchance by sympathy to make amends
For isolation, loneliness and pain,
Robert and Agnes welcomed o'er the main.

Manhood has claimed the contour of his brow,—
Youth leaves him on its daisy threshold now;
New scenes broad from its vine-wreathed lintels
          spread,
He walks beneath with fragrance on his head,
Throwing late-woven garlands lightly down,
In bold pursuit of hope's alluring crown.
Love with ambition speeds his buoyant feet,
Unmingled, sphered alone, each power complete;
If one be deep, then is the other strong;
For true it is love's wakened powers belong
To later days in some maturing hearts,
Who feel not all their might till youth departs.

His father's parting benediction said,
His mother's kiss returned with absent dread
Of hidden dangers, while the younger band
Of wistful sisters clinging to his hand,
Draw down his head in turn with fond embrace,
Commingling tear with tear, with solemn face,
And half-repenting thought, one vernal day
From home's protecting band he breaks away.

While parts the spray around a brave ship's prow,
Behold him silent o'er the gunwale bow!
Do dreams of future glory fill his brain?
Does aught admonish love's approaching pain?
Or in the pride of love's parental dower,
Still mourns his heart the tender parting hour?
The gems that sparkle in the deeps beneath

Recall the dew-drops trembling on the heath
When aimless childhood trode the grass of May
In salutation of the new-born day.
In those declining eddies, one by one,
Succeeding, circling, whirling, quickly gone,
He whom no mighty rush had taught Earth's strife,
Beheld the mimic waves of mortal life ;—
But break not now his reveries ; the ship
Is bounding forward with majestic dip ;
Soon breezy days and nights of moon-light bloom
Waft Oscar far from Scotland, friends and home.

'Columbia ! My soul approves thy righteous pride
Thy noble right to emigration's tide,—
Thou green-earth-bosom,—nurse for honest toil,
The people's sovereignty, the tyrant's foil !
But Scotia ! thou immortal in thy song,
The glory of high bards,—to thee belong
Feelings most ardent, tributes of thy sons ;
Now o'er thy lochs and hills my fancy runs,—
The purple mist that vails them from the sky
Gleams with old memories ; there heart and eye
Gaze eloquent with homage ; truth is bright
In time's unfolding of thy deeds of light :
And where, o'er all the Earth, my soul, O where
Does nature so invigorate its air
That from the poet's lyre diviner song
Has thrilled the muses' rapt devoted throng?'

A wilderness of domes, and spires, and walls,

Toward which the bark is bent, now calls
Him from his reverie ;—to ripples blue,
And foam-white surges, whispers he ' adieu :'—
The anchor cast, the weary sails are furled
Where thrift and commerce hail the Western World
He steps upon the firm unrivaled shores
That foster freedom's growing strength, and pours
Emotion's tribute from a grateful heart,
Whose beating pulse is yet untrained to art.

Scarce time the wondrous city to survey,
He speeds upon his love-directed way :—
Tis June : beneath New-England's sun of gold,
Lilac, and rose, and snow-ball blooms unfold ;
He thinks the vales—green footstools of the hills—
As fair as aught whereon the dew distils ;
Their pine-crowned summits seem as near to heaven
As barren crags Loch Lomond's storms have riven.
Each peaceful habitation chains his view,
Each village spire, with admiration new,
And he exclaims, ' the pure, the true, the kind,
Contentment's precious treasures here shall find !'

Removed, in green luxurious solitude,
Sequestered from the clustering hamlet brood,
Beside a gentle curve the river lined,
'Glen cottage' smiled to cheer his anxious mind :
A mountain brooklet near it sought the tide
Of Housatonic, stream of Indian pride ;

And towards the East its low arched doorway met
Morn breaking o'er the cloudy parapet :
Alighting from the stage, he turned to seek,
With wondrous eyes and story-telling cheek,
A 'bower' by flowering vines and boughs entwined,
Where fair Allien in summer hours reclined :—
Below a knoll a pathway soon he found
Whose curvings toward the sparkling brooklet wound
Which, where it rushed more eagerly to meet
The river's breast, disclosed the maid's retreat
Its low, o'erhanging boughs the waters laved,
Around it lay a path by pebbles paved,
And green festoons described the rustic door,
Which passing, Oscar pressed the mossy floor.
New scenes held no rebuke that memory claimed
The past so sacred ; present angels named
Advancing joys—new ties that soon will bind
The roseate hours to leave all shade behind.
The child of many prayers and training just,
Not then did he forget the holy trust
A grateful heart preserves :—He rose, imbued
With pure resolves, by earnest prayer subdued.

'My cousin comes,' he thought, 'each sunset hour
Alone and pensive to this sylvan bower ;
I'll leave a simple token for her eye,
And hither in the day's decline I'll hie :'
He wrote : 'Thy mother's and thy father's friend

2*   C

Unasked, has ventured here his steps to bend,
Coming from far ;—thou wilt rebuke him not?
O meet me then in this enchanted spot,
When sunset softens on the summit hills,
And shadows troop along the deepening rills ;
Here ours shall be the pledge of friendship true.'
A curling tendril of the Virgin's Bower,*
To tie the note with leaf and snowy flower ;
Laid on the maple seat the strange boquet,
And turning, slow retraced his thoughtful way
Until the humble village inn he found,
Wearied, to rest at noon in sleep profound.

The royal sun gleamed in the purple west,
Where vailing cloud-folds urged the day to rest ;
Hushed notes of life, the herald sounds of night,
Gave Oscar's sanguine heart a new delight,
And now with eager pace his footsteps fly
Toward Allien's bower in charmed credulity :
The way not half as long as first it seemed,
While yet adjacent hills in pale rays gleamed,
In flush of hope and dignity of pride,
He stands again the unique tryst beside.

Soon floating in the gentle evening breeze,
Approaching him a snow-white scarf he sees,
When noiseless, in a thicket near he hides.

*Clemat's Virginiaua.

And almost guilty his own breathing chides.
Oh, love from infancy is part
Of man's existence ; shed upon his heart
Like mist-rains to sustain the flowers
That bless parental and fraternal bowers ;—
In childhood, it out-flows like fountain-showers,
More full, defined, more tangible, and warm
When too its action is a natural charm :
In youth it falls in periods like dews,
But 'mid the sunshine, when the prism's hues
Gleam from each bright division, but defy
The prescience of the most prophetic eye :
In manhood 'tis a passion all controlling ;
In age, serenity and strength, consoling.

Allien passed by with joyous, dancing air,—
Unseen, he saw she was supremely fair.
The carols of the answering birdlings free
She sang, and gushed her notes etherially ;
Almost she seemed a muse of harmony,
A wing-borne fairy, as she brushed aside
The lacing boughs,—a nymph of wood or tide.

Pleasure ! Art thou mere absence of distress ?
The sunlight, not the living orb ? Dost bless
But transiently, withdrawing, that the shade
May fix upon the beauty thou hast made ?
Art thou a personated power of mind
Whose office, thoughts or words have ne'er defined ?
Not these, yet num'rous are thy images

As leaves that clothe the boughs of forest trees;
And varying in degree, as life descends
From God to angels, virtuous man to fiends:
Thou hast a radiant climax in the hour
When dignate man embraces beauty's power;
Clasping with condescending grace the sprite,
Vanquished, though unacknowledged, by delight!

Arousing from a sweet, new trance of thought,
To make his presence known, young Oscar sought,
And while the billet lingered in her hand,
She bowed to see her cousin near her stand:
Then slight as pinkwhite roses flush anew
When o'er them gleams the sunset's red'ning hue,
Her cheeks were heightened, and her parted lips
No carmine bud or blossom might eclipse,
Gave music sweeter to his charmed ear
Than all the strains his memory could transfer.—

'If Oscar of Glenwayne, I now may greet,
Most welcome to my father's home retreat;—
From childhood I have heard my cousin's name,—
Too happy, I respond to friendship's claim!'
Then with a trusting but reserving mien,
She placed her yielding hand his own between;
He gently raised the snowy pledge and prest
Revering lips, then laid it on his breast.

Now seated by her side, the moments fly
Too swiftly, till the darkening shadows lie,

Deep, trembling with the ripples, and no bird
Trilling faint notes on dream-land's verge is heard;
When not abruptly breaking from the tale
His words have woven of his native vale,
Or glen, o'erhung by precipice and crag,
The terror of the foiled and hunted stag,
The pride of one bold clan, who valiant, know,
If needed, a sure refuge from the foe ;
She rises, by the way the waters move,
To lead him to the cottage home of love,
Beside the garden wall and through the gate,
Where in the moonlit porch her parents wait :—
Unconscious movements and inquiring eyes
Betray their sudden, undisguised surprise :—
'My father, cousin Oscar ;—mother dear,
Behold one kindred friend has found us here!'
The twain advance with open arms to greet
A brother's child ;—they meet as true hearts meet.

'My boy! thou'rt welcome here ! Thy mother's eye
Is thine. Thy brow, like her's, is arched and high,—
I see the classic profile of her face ;
The outlines of thy father's form I trace :—
How cam'st thou, boy, to seek this alien shore,
To find thy long-lost uncle's lowly door?'

He ceased :—The matron spoke with gentle word,—
The deeps of youth's uncovered stream were stirred :
'Oscar, dear child of Scotia wild and blest,
Beneath whose heather-turf my parents rest,

Whose gowans are the brightest, and whose braes
Were friendly in my sad complaining days ;
Whose ingle-sides are shrines of peace and truth,
Which gave their radiance to my hopeful youth,—
What spirit sent thee hitherward to cheer
These wanderers from home and kindred dear ?—
Blessings fall lightly on thy noble head !
Life's softest paths thy feet perpetual tread !'

The youth possessed a glowing soul ; a will
Subservient ever to deep feeling's thrill ;
But eloquence of speech he boasted not,
And for this welcome ne'er to be forgot,
He to his aunt but courteously replied,
Still standing by his lovely cousin's side :—

'O, gentle aunt, if pleasure's thought is thine,
Inspired as by reunion, more is mine,
And tenderly I thank thy memory sweet
For picturing all my love of home would greet !'

We number . not those weeks so free from care
And cloud, that hours and days uncounted were ;
Nor talk of admiration, beauty, worth,
Man's gentleness of mind,—all best on Earth
Living in man and woman :—there's one theme
Sustained by all, some hearts call not, 'a dream ;'
By its own name we say *love* dared to own
Secret belief that two fond hearts were one.
Then came the parting hour, almost concealing

Joy's painted landscape, scarce hope's torch revealing:
Two years must pass ere Oscar claim his bride,
And take her to the manor's ingle-side !—
The active world between the lovers rushed,
And by its din affection's tones were hushed.

O reader, hast thou severed trembling strings
Which bound in love thy weary spirit's wings;
Fibres so bliss-bestowing, yet so fine,
Linking another's sweeter soul to thine;
Thrilling from pulse to pulse when barely swayed
By world-rude questionings; if pained, allayed
By nought of healing that the world may boast,
Yet cured by one warm kiss, when lips are lost
To individual possession, scaling
Commingled hearts anew with truth's revealing;—
Severed by cold, unimaged space, though brief,
By hope's bought promise, fear's indulged relief!
Then knowest thou what 'parting' means to those
Who loving thus fail ever to disclose
Experience to a novice :—Heaven protect
Me from such pain I would not recollect!

The future laird on ocean's cradling breast,
Dim grow the shores, dissolving in the west;
Columbia disappears ; his silent gaze
Far round finds nought but formless haze ;
Blue waves beneath, blue space above, night's stars,
Days solitary orb, horizon bars:
These only break a long monotony,

Till weeks are passed, and storm is on the sea.

'Man over-board!'   Like thunder breaks the cry,
But waves are wild; the night is dark, winds high,
And few the ears that hear the awful tale,—
A life is swallowed by the vengeful gale!
No arm to rescue, never known his grave,—
Deep, dark, untroubled by the lower wave ;—
The sailor's weeping mother, wife, or child,
Shall never, when the airs of spring are mild,
Plant in that death-cold, isolated spot,
Pale violets or blue 'forget-me-not.'
The creaking ship careens and bounds and moans ;
The waters roar in dread affrighting tones ;—
Anon there flashes, not the lightning's glare,
But shooting stars amid the billows are!
Bright phosphorescence penetrates the deep,—
It waken's not the poor lost sailor's sleep ;
Nor all the rattle of the rigging calls
Him from the lower ocean's silent halls.
Quickly he sank, his leaden journey brief,
Unmindful of the sea-weed's mesh, or reef
Of populous white coral cities :— Gone,
Until the judgment day, to rest—alone.

Diffusive halos from the storied Past,
Through memory's aid were round Dumbarton cast,
Enkindling by the wanderer's return
Ardor that but in patriot breasts may burn.
He pauses on the silver-limpid Clyde,

And sweeps his eye o'er mount and moor-field wide ;—
Upwelling tears of gratitude and joy
Unite man's impulse to the former boy :—
'O, never may my steps, a pilgrim, roam
From thee my fatherland, my glorious home!
Most eloquent, heroic, truth declares
High deeds inspired by thy pure mountain airs ;—
In loyal hearts that swell in pride for thee,
There lives the innate strength of liberty!—
Thou future! show by page or magic glass,
My life by God decreed, with thee to pass!
Shed radiance on its brinks of danger ; sweep
Their clustering roses down, lest I may sleep
Too near destruction's pit, and in despair
Discover but too late I'm rolling there!
Ah! wisdom hath such fearful power withheld,
Lest many a hope of virtue be dispelled,
And present time, inert with clouds of woe,
Hold back progressive life, or still its flow,
Annihilating faith with double gloom,
Making bright hope a shadow of the tomb.
Forbid it God,—the impious wish exprest
To fathom secrets of thy Triune breast ;—
The humble acquiescent of thy will,
My eyes unveiled, my destiny fulfil.'

Thought's course is changed : with vigor speed his feet
Toward ancient walls in view, where waters meet
Around the castle's base, and shine away

Far north, where waits the bosom of Achray.
We may not count the joy his presence gives
When friends at home behold that Oscar lives.

One after one the zodiacal train
With each peculiar dress robed hill and plain;—
June roses died; red clover blooms grew scar;
Dim leaves foretold the autumn of the year
When bright eyed asters wore the varying tinge
Of distant skies upon their starry fringe.
Afar along the hills the crimson glow
Of dying verdure faded, dull and slow,
The evening airs spread cooler round the rill,
And in the pastures morning dews were chill.
Rich fields of golden grain above the glen
Had ripened, and were stored in barn and pen;
No more was seen the tasselled crowns of maize,—
They were dethroned amid the August days,
Their yellow treasures for the future stored
Where plenty smiled upon the shining hoard.

Its breath absorbed by the o'erpowering blast,
Grand Autumn to the unknown mist land passed;
Wrinkled and brown a few lone leaves were left,
Trembling on boughs December had bereft.
Allien is lonely now; she hails the star
Each night which shines o'er Oscar's path afar,—
Arcturus 'mong his dimmer suns, benign,
Above the dark-robed firs,— a gem divine,—

In bright companionship, though lower down,
With Cynosure upon the zenith's crown,
And oft when Luna's silver draperies shed
A magic radiance on her curtained bed,
Her eye-lids, like half-yielding sentries, start
At some new strain love wakens from her heart.

O, Love is like a wandering bird
   In search of sunny skies ;
It echoes far, its echoes heard,
   Then echo-like it flies !

Unmeasured in the flight of mind,
   No rest it deigns to claim ;
It roams afar its mate to find,
   And asks no boon of Fame.

O, name not Love a fearless child—
   Remembrancer of fears !—
Dead leaflets show where roses smiled,—
   On these love sheds its tears.

Thou vernal consciousness of life,
   Too blooming long to last,—
Sweet lisping tenderness of strife,
   Preceding sorrow's blast !

Allien, recall thy roving dreams,
   Thy heart needs rest again ;
Prepare to meet revulsive streams,
   To nurse affection's pain !

The wind blew shrill one cloudy day;
Within the cot a sufferer lay,
Whose tide of life was ebbing slow,—
Well-nigh congealed its purple flow;
Now watchers o'er the couch bend low
And words of faint farewell are said
Ere death rests on a father's head.

That mother taught by years of toil
From heart-rebellion to recoil,
While griefs their shadows round her bind,
Has one resource for heart and mind:
Bright Faith illuminates the tomb,
And bears her spirit from its gloom,
And on each image of the dead
Does love divine its glory shed.

Allien beneath this weight of grief
First flutters like an aspen leaf;
Unused to sorrow's crushing air,
Her prayers are breathings of despair:
Her hopes of bliss are all undone
That he, her father dear, is gone;
The one heart left her now to love
Is mild and faithful as the dove,
And tenderly her being clings
To her protecting mother's wings.

As time moved on with noiseless stride,
Nearer to Spring's unfolding pride,

Before some faggots blazing bright
They sat alone one chilly night.
Allien the silence broke :—'The time
Is long since Oscar left our clime !
Four dreary months, and yet no word
To me has come,—no spirit bird !
My heart in this is doubly sad,—
Hopes all too bright at first I had ;—
I sometimes fear his mute form sleeps
In ocean's dark unyielding deeps.'

'My daughter, find thy fullest joy in prayer,
Nor ever of the future hope too much :
Suffer not doubt to darken present good ;
Committed to thy Savior's care, thy days
Shall each unite—a golden link to bind
Thy thoughts of happiness,—immortal hopes,'—

The post-boy broke the earnest scene,—
'A letter here for Miss Allien !'
She caught the treasure with a smile,—
Unconscious tears gushed forth the while ;
She quickly broke the scarlet seal
Love's faithful story to reveal,
Anxious and tenderly she read ;
Hope burned anew,—*he* was not dead.

'Allien ! I met thee long ago in thought—
In childhood's rosy morn, before the sun

Of youth dispelled the infant dews that lay
On every reaching tendril of my heart,
Shining, each one a sphere of crystal joy !
And these were dreams of day as well as night :—
My mother's nursery tales, in glowing hues,
Drew pictures of a little blue-eyed girl
Who lived the wide, wide field of waters o'er,
In a far land, so vast 'twas little known,
Whose father hence had roamed in other times,
The still dear scion of our noble line.

   I thought I loved my cousin then, and wild,
Sweet fancies filled my brain ; I thought to see
That little one in future days.   In time
I thought to find those flowery wilds, and bring
The bloom most fair to our paternal home.

    Swift years flew by ; I found the treasure, Bird
    Of Paradise to me ; mine, only mine.

Kind fairies ! make a plume of every tress,
And then my love will fly to me.   She would
Not pause till o'er the hills around this glen,
To rest her fluttering wings, impatient still ;
Caledonia's air would give them glorious hues,
And my own breast her panting heart restore.
Now come ; and on the heather's bank I'll meet
My bird of love !   Our clasping selves, ordained
For one pure end, one living sphere of bliss,
Shall move toward perfect being—life eterne.

   'Tis long since we were parted, love !   I passed
My homeward journey safely ;—As I breathe

My native air I deem it purer than
Before my wandering ;—Life is strong ;—I wait
Sweet tidings, words of tenderness and truth
From thee, my own !—I am forever thine.'

December's Borean breezes blow,
Dead leaves are sepulchered in snow :
Among the tufts of gloomy pines
Funereal wail the spirit-winds ; ,
Proud Nature Summer's requiem sings,
And on the earth its vendure flings.
Spring, Summer, Autumn, passed away,
And sweet Allien this many a day
Has hoped, and sighed, and mourned in vain,
For she has learned the fatal pain
Of dread suspense that quells the fire
Anticipation and desire
May feed in hearts that early love,
When nought untoward may reprove,
While as mid ruins, one dark thought
Mingling one shadow more, has brought
A chillier air, an added gloom,
Presaging sorrow in her home.
Maternal joy and love and worth
Briefly illume its lonely hearth ;
For paler grow her mother's cheeks,—
Her languid step a tale bespeaks
Which had her eye no power to read,
Her heart were happier indeed.

When gloomy sounds the branches bare
Are beating 'gainst the frosty air,—
While rest the streams in silver chains,
And freezing drops glaze o'er the panes,—
When hemlock boughs before the sky
In outlines dark sway gloomily ;—
When night has drawn its inner vail,
And stars if seen are glimmering pale,
Before their ruddy open fire
They feed the intellect's desire.

Allien, with gently varying mood,
Reads of the wise, the great, the good,
Whose lives in grandeur thread the Past,
And bright, or soft reflections cast
Along the ever-rolling stream
In whose deep current thought and dream
Become engulfed, from age to age,
Till history reveals the page.

They delve in old Castile romance,
In tales of red crusader's lance,
Read Cœur-de-Lion's short-lived fame,
Or how Columbus won a name ;—
Of mystic times of Rome and Greece;
Of oriental wars and peace ;
Melancthon, Luther, Cromwell bold,
And Semiramis' reign of old ;
Of Switzer peaks ; of Scottish fell ;
Of Alfred, Wallace, Bruce and Tell ;

Of Alexander's young campaign,
And Cæsar's glory-thirsting reign ;
Of Henry Eighth's remorseless part,
To marry wives, and break each heart;
Of Cleopatra, Egypt's queen,
With splendid, cold and haughty mien,
Whose life and suicidal end
Dark shadows to her memory lend ;
And of that gentle Roman wife*
Who gave the noble Gracchi life.

And, when the nights were calm and still,
When moonbeams lit each snow-crowned hill,
And winter shone in beauty cold,—
When back was prest each curtain's fold
That in might flow the lustrous stream,
The songs of bards became their theme.

They almost hear the breathing lyre
    Of Avon sound again,
Or feel wild Ossian's wandering fire,
    And Spencer's holy strain.

Quaint Francis Quarles they knew and read,
    With songs of Scotland old,
Which pictured how her warriors bled
    In fray, and battle, bold.

---

* Cornelia Gracchus, daughter of Scipo Africanus.

3   D

From sage old Homer's classic tide
   They learned how Grecians warred :—
They loved the harp of Israel, tried
   By David, matchless bard !

Petrarca's numbers thrilled anew
   Life's wearied, languid lyre
And hope revived as Dante true
   . Re-kindled love's dim fire.

Mild Tasso, like his native skies,
   Lent heaven's pure glow to thought,
And from blind Milton's poet eyes
   Flashed gleams their spirits caught.

Thus Winter passed away ; mild Spring began
To woo the blossoms forth ; new waters ran
In liquid light and free ;—last year's decay
Oblivious grew beneath the smile of May.
   Glen-Cottage stood in sunshine, but within
There lurked a shadow : one sweet face grew thin,
One form its slower step betrayed ; some eyes
Brightened like stars of their own native skies.

Dear Mother, why so oft that tearful check
When pressed on mine ! Not now as once you speak :
Your sweet caress is still all tenderness,
But oh ! those mournful tears my hopes oppress.
Each kiss I leave upon your calm pale brow,
Seems one the less cold fate will there allow ;—

I shrink, yet if an orphan's lot be mine
The Lord forbid my stricken heart to pine,
Must I without one parent's gentle care,
Endure alone the world's unfriendly air?'
   O'ercome by sorrow, here she ceased the strain
And silence but increased the mutual pain,
Till words incited from the mother's lips,
Like shades penumbral in the sun's eclipse,
A darkening circle seemed more clear to bind
Around the faith-star of her daughter's mind.

   'My child, 'twas ever thy lost father's care,
And mine, to plant the germs of holiness
Within thy virgin heart for future bloom;
To give thee early knowledge of commands
The wise Creator has imposed on all
The creatures of his power and love. Thou art
Responsible for every act,—for thought
Of sin, if cultivated or indulged ;
And such are enemies to happiness.
This world is not a place for hopeless gloom ;
A heart desiring good, a life of prayer,
And sweet submission to the laws of life,
Shall reap the fruits of peace—perpetual smiles
   Thou art a dear and duteous child ;—some pangs
Assail my erring heart when pressed with thoughts
That soon my failing form must yield its breath
To angel ministry, to conduct safe,
In all its disembodied, fluttering sense

Of mysteries immortal, opening strange
But, oh! I will submissively resign
My darling to the orphan's Friend ;—Few years
At most I'll meet thee, dear, in Paradise:
To God I trust thy promise ;—For some high
And useful end my only child will live.

Be true to Oscar.   When the time expires,
Thy nuptials consummated, freely go
Where e'er thy husband's way of life may lead ;
Where e'er thy husband's home, that home be thine;
Thy duties be thy joys, with cheerful step,
Whether in humble or exalted walk—
Let all thy acts be true to woman's trust.

Sometimes, Allien, does love forget its truth,
When all its early glow grows dim and chill ;
When new and dazzling pictures charm the heart ;—
O cultivate the violets of faithfulness,—
Let no suspicious weed their growth obscure!

Work faithfully, wait patiently, and God
Thy destiny shall mark and guide, nor thou
Canst change, nor still the flutter of one leaf
Of life, or hue of one sweet flower of joy,
Unaided by Omnipotence and prayer ;—
May wisdom be reflected in thy soul!'

In still mysterious fall to Earth,
Like thoughts that own a heavenly birth,
A mantle draped the ground one night
In soft surprise of flaky white.

Each porous, fair, adhering part
Was fashioned with unlettered art;
In one pure vesture all combined,
As thoughts weave textures for the mind.

All unexpectedly it fell
When vernal bloom lit up the dell;
When balmy airs had lent their breath
To frosts benighted on the heath ;—

While May was whispering of June,
But ere the earnest gaze of noon
It melted silently away,
Symbol of beauty's swift decay.

Glen-Cottage, ere that day was gone,
Sent forth a deeply sorrowing moan ·—
As soft as melt the vernal snows,
As dew falls on a chaliced rose,
As calm as floats the evening's breath
A mother passed away in death.
    A few low words and all was still
As winter-chains may bind a rill ;
In sweet arrangement on her breast
Her small cold hands were laid to rest;
But wakened by the sun of Heaven,
A glad immortal action given,
Her spirit soared above the skies
Completer powers to exercise ;—
She passed in faith serene away,—

  Her night of life awoke to-day.

  'My mother! Art thou gone! O, speak!
Alas! there's coldness on thy cheek.
Dear mother, look once more, once more,
Upon thy loving child—once more!
No, no, my heart, it cannot be;
These eyes will ope no more on me.
Remains there in this clouded world
A guardian for thine orphan girl?'—
Then burst her grief in tears like rain,
And failed her tongue to end the strain,
While o'er the lifeless form she bent
In sorrow's crushed abandonment,
Till soft and gentle arms removed
Her from the one she best had loved.

The village of the dead!—What solemn air,
What silent gloom its habitudes declare!
There swaying daisies have a paler crown;
There bends the Babylonian willow down;
Carnation blooms have there a sickly smell;
There grasses an ephemeral lesson tell,
And ever with the grave-yard's gloom
Associates the brier's* pale-hued bloom.
  O, I remember, when a truant child.
I dared not pluck the berries red and wild

---

* Rosa rubiginosa

The strawberries ripening on each deathly mound,
The consecrated place was so profound.
Ah! children have strange senses unexplained
Whose influence is after long retained ;
Call them not vagaries, nor passing dreams,
They're life's reflections on its morning streams

Mournfully, mournfully, tolls the village bell ;
Slow dying murmurs sink in copse and and dell ;—
Now slowly, slowly, winds a measured train
Around the hill, above the river plane,
Nearer and nearer to the black-edged gates,
Where narrow and damp a hollow grave awaits
Ah! who has fastened wide the portals back ?
Did spectral Death precede the mourners' track ?
Among the mossy tablets lettered old,
Where life's brief histories are quaintly told,
The mute procession winds ; the *bearers* pause ;—
A hand has oped the Book of Love and Laws,
And heads uncovered, list with solemn trust,—
'All flesh is grass,' and, ' dust returns to dust,'
Pronounced by reverent lips. A prayer arose,
And then a sound that every mourner knows :
Dull, rattling clods upon the coffin spread,
And rising winds mourn sadder—for the dead

Amid the ills that life's footsteps attend
The young and pure may never want a friend
The orphan in the pastor's cottage finds
The warm devotion of congenial minds ;

Benignant love and sweet untiring care
Protect her from the world's unhallowed air;
Parental and fraternal love disclose
New pleasures, softening all her early woes,
While as from each departed dear one's tomb
New flowers give promise of celestial bloom.

'Helen,' adopted sister of Allien,
Was beautiful as Sparta's erring queen,
Whom Trojan Paris with delusive art
Allured from Menelaus' home and heart.
Her eyes were changeful in their brilliant hue,
Dark flashing, hazel-brown, or azure-blue,
Piquant in smile, and liquid in repose,
Kindling when song from other lips arose
A fleecy cloudlet was her silken hair,   .
Whose floating meshes, kissed by sunbeams, were
Entanglements delightful round the hand
Possessed through aid of some enchanter's wand;
So like the skies of April,—tear-suffused!
Her brow by frowns o'er-cast,—her smiles unused
Through transient grief;—a sunbeam, or kind tone,
The spell was broken, and the shadow gone!
Of mediocral grade her lively mind,
Her heart was all affection if combined,
The sweet approvals flattery interweaves,
Trembling in happiness like breath-stirred leaves.
The captive of anticipations bright,
She ill could bear their shading into night,

Nor calmly walked where disappointment led,
So rich the feasts on which her fancy fed.

A brother's heart!—O, tis a holy shrine,
Where kindred love is near to love divine !
Unselfish, free from passion's dross, as dew
Is pure at dawn, as noon-day skies are blue.
The cascade's foam is free, so this from weight
Of all dark mixture ; it can ne'er create
Regret, distrust, or weariness, or sigh ;
And more, a brother's love may never die.
'T was new. Allien to its consoling power
Was passive as the mountain hair-bell flower,
When wandering sunbeams find its purple cheek,
And cause its own pure radiance to speak.

Adoption !—More than natural ties 'tis strong
To bind congenial hearts like notes in song,
When every stir of thought and feeling owns
Melodious brotherhood of dulcet tones ;
When spirit floats with spirit, as one wave
Of love's eternal tide their free hopes lave ;
When just to feel we know another's bliss
Is full enough for kindred happiness.
Affinities of mind are stars in dreams,
So rare few souls discern and feel their beams ;
One sinless pair, one Eden, and one fall,
Have brought the hope,—the seeming to us all.

Warm Summer floats again her languid air,
   Through tissued cloud and silent space, as sails
The pearly nautilus on waters, where
   Hushed ripples cover ocean's slumbering gales.

High Nature's worshipers may tune their lyres,
   Of joy's ideal profusion rapturous sing,
To mitigate life's wild and feverish fires,
   While love-flushed fancy may repose her wing.

The artist, faithful to his given powers,
   May roam the wide expanse of hill and plain,
With fond allurements win the rosy hours,
   And reproduce the forms of beauty's train.

The poet's sweet perceptions newly wake,—
   Mysterious alcoves lure his radiant dreams,
Where subtile forms ambrosial feasts partake,
   And hope quaff's love's exhilarating streams.

From the deserted cot across the stile,
   Beyond the hamlet's bound, along the brook,
Allien's adopted home was just a mile,—
   One early morn her footsteps sought the nook ;
One mute companion of her lonely way,
   The favorite dog whose speaking eyes surveyed
With instinct bright, and sympathetic play,
   The gentle features of the thoughtful maid.
Where thriving shrubs in tangled masses grew
   Around her once frequented, well-pruned bower,

With casual pause, and sad, slow step she drew,
   Her memory quickening with grief's painful power.
Withdrawing from her breast a treasured page,
   She pressed some foliage down which caught her
      tear,
And sought a few calm moments to engage,—
   No eye but one from heaven beheld her there.
'T was Oscar's message, and the only one,
   Tear-stained, read often, dear and always new;
The period of betrothal now was gone,
   His step came not,—her heart believed him true,—
O when will love its early hopes resign?
   When young affection's tendrils cease to weave
Illumined wreaths which oft so briefly shine,
   Fading a fragile ruin but to leave!

Behold a living drama of this age!
   The last brave act will soon forever close;
Its stormy scenes and glittering icy stage
   Were laid mid solitudes of Arctic snows.
Aurora Borealis arched the dome,
   Darting its painted changing lustres down
To gild the region of the north-winds home,
   Where Winter never doffs his diamond crown:
The throngs who gazed looked far o'er land and sea,
   Science a fadeless flag o'er all unfurled,
While noble FRANKLIN's knell met solemnly
   Applauding echoes trembling through the world.
No gold weighed down the balance when his fate

Was undetermined in the lapse of years,
For Lady Franklin, rich in love's estate,
   Still hoped and sought through all her gloomy fears.
A woman true, her tireless efforts prove
   A spectacle for every age, sublime;
Th' eternal constancy of holy love
   Which braves the icebergs and the seas of time.

Now sunbeams passing from a special bound,
   Oft marked before, are signal for return;
Allien, roused by the purling streamlet's sound,
   Shuts back these memories in her heart's deep urn;
Her trembling lips grow calm; a precious sense
   Of God's protecting and supernal will
Becomes her tender spirit's firm defense,—
   Divinely given pledge for future ill.

She walks the garden path; the broken gate
   No more a barrier its form conceals
Neath wild exuberance—a weedy state;
   The bushy flat still here and there reveals
The serrate leaflets of the damask rose,
   Craving of unpruned nature its consent,
A few more buds and blossoms to disclose,
   Though on the desert air their sweets be spent.
She lifts the rusted latchet, slowly through
   The dusky entry walks and meets still airs
Impregnated with damps and vapors blue;—
   Each wall a high and dim festooning wears,—
Not Gobelin fabric, fabulous in price,

But hung, as if in mockery of taste,
With cobwebs, woven in looms of strange device
By noiseless beings, and in secret placed.
She sounds her parents' names in failing tones,
The haunted roof responds in echoes drear ;
The spirit of the blackened chimney moans,—
Remembrance sighs ; love murmurs, 'they're not
here !'
Her steps are backward turned; a long 'farewell'
Escapes her lips : 'No more my feet shall tread
This hallowed ground,— too mournful weighs the
spell,—
Where e'er I roam my heart may weep its dead.'

Cheery the gambols of the dog; from sight
The sun behind the evening's vesture bowed ;
Birds sought their coverts for the coming night,—
Soon all is mute within its mystic shroud :
As one by one the burnished stars appear,
To crown the dome's o'ershadowing expanse,
The world is sleeping ; heaven seems more near,—
Shaded and shining, waiting morning's glance.

Bidding good-night to hope and the celestial host,
Allien sinks soon and sweetly to repose ;
And now she wanders on a darkened coast,
Unconscious how the risen moonlight glows ;
The roar of many swelling waves combined
Sends mornful music o'er the distant leas ;
Afar across the waters, lone, defined,

A meteor—a glimmering light she sees.
It sinks, anon it rises from the tide ;
 Each time it seems more near, more brightly shines ;
Its flickering gleams disclose the ocean wide,
 But far before no pebbly shore defines.
She stands transfixed, her straining eyes intent,
 And knows nor what, nor why the potent charm ;—
Now o'er the sea the sky seems darker bent,—
 A strengthening breeze is herald for the storm.
Along the lea, among the pine-boughs dark,
 A lounder wail is sounding, o'er and o'er ;
More often disappears the meteor-spark,
 The angry tide is sweeping up the shore ;
Hoarse thunders in the darkness roll away,
 And fearless Tritons rise in self defense ;
But soon allied, they with the billows play,
 Lest Neptune's frowns betray his ire intense.
No slavish fears assail her courage there ;
 Still firm she stands and all the storm defies,
Beholds the light again to leeward bear,—
 It comes more near ; it rises to the skies.

Then rose the curtains of the hall of sleep ;—
 The maiden opes her wondering eyes to view
The calm and starry night, almost to weep
 O'er visions waking sense would not renew.
The world is silent ;—Midnight reigns ;
 Within her windows, all unshaded, falls
A flood of silver bloom the moon sustains ;

The hills stand guarding all the dells and vales;
Soft slumbers soon again her eyelids close,—
Now undisturbed her conciousness is lost,
Till o'er the Eastern heights break sunny glows,
Whose shades withdrew as Day the valley crost.

Morning !—'Tis said the shades of evening seem
Propitious most to love's imparting dream;
That sighs are softer then, and kisses mute,—
Love's ripened figs—unblighted, timely fruit;
That whispers have more meaning when the stir
Of life is hushed; that gentler, lovelier,
Is beauty's cheek and brow, in night's pale wreath;
And so 't is fitting time for love to breathe
Its monosyllable requests and vows,
When hands and lips unite, and brows meet brows.
    But morning hours for love of mine; when care
May not oppress one ripple thought may bear;
When weariness is an unmeaning sound
To hearts all music, sleep a word profound.
    So thought young 'Mortimer.'— A shaded seat
Had checked the wandering of some happy feet;
And while the river mirrored light and morn,
And redder grew the berries of the thorn,
He prest the maiden's hand and sought her eyes ;—
The rainbow wreath that in one sunbeam lies,
A crystal prism surely will reveal,
And while the morning zephyr seeks to steal
The lily from her cheek and kiss her eye,

He speaks of love—not love's fraternity.

Serene has been their converse; children each
Of favoring Nature, lessons she would teach
With all her beauty, mystery of form,
Wildness and freedom, sleeping strength, or storm,
Find quick acceptance in their gentle souls,
Mingling as wave to wave together rolls
Congenial in enjoyment, treasuring
Each one alike the happiness they bring.

'Sweet friend, our parting hour is near at hand,
When I must hasten to a far-off land,
Crossing the distant Mississippi's flood,
Where savage wild, dim wilderness, and wood,
Must be my portion, happiness and home;—
And must I there with no companion roam?
That we do love each other, nature owns,—
Let one sweet word bear witness through thy tones!
A missionary's wife !   Such offering speaks
No splendid state for thee, but true love seeks
From my devoted spirit to sustain
Thy trusting heart in every care or pain;
O, more than friend !   No words can tell
How well I love thee,—'tis almost too well !'

Silent a moment;—'twas a strange new charm
That clasped her being with his gentle arm ;
She did not know 'twas more than all before.
Thought hastened far—beyond Atlantic's shore,—
Long months, the fever of suspense, the tears

In silence fallen, unbestowing years,
To love's solicitude no answer gave;
Back from the past, back o'er the blue-deep wave,
Her fretted spirit almost willing came,
Just outside Eden, breathing a new name,
Reaching for new-blown flowers, that o'er the wall
Of maidenly reserve escaped the thrall;—
Such silence seals affiance,—not alway,
And light fast streaming toward the noon of day
Wakes one from bliss, and one to duty's line,
She whispering, 'sister, only such I'm thine.'

'My love, alas! misled by its own light,
A meteor to break upon my future's night
Again and oft again, when thoughts of thee
Through sacrificial toil sigh tenderly!
Farewell, my own! before the morrow's dawn,
Ere yet thy slippered feet have prest the lawn,
Friends, home and thee, I leave, to meet no more,
Perchance till Earth and time's receding shore
Are to the winging soul a fleck, a vapor dim;
Their memories like bell-tones lost, or hymn
Of melody and discord, long ago;
Yes, thus—alone—in silence, thus I go; -
But some day, dearest, I shall call thee—mine;—
A hidden diamond ne'er forgets to shine.'

'Hail, mystic Night! Time's reaching strand
Bounds far away thy shadowy land,

Where all the future's pregnant days
Sleep, warmed with hope's half latent rays !

'I love thy silent mysteries
As well as day which dazzling flies,
Expansive from the burning fount,
Embracing sky, and plain, and mount.

'Float on unseen, ye soundless airs,
While night her sable drapery wears ;
Vibrate from mountain hight to dell,
And cradle still the fancy's spell !

'Ye rivulets, in soft emprise
While now ye meet from Dian's eyes
A tide of lustres dreaming down,
Through quiet shades move stiller on !

'While Nature's heart is still like death,
Ye leafy branches, wake no breath,
Nor let your birdling brood prolong.
Aloud one note of dreamy song.

'Ye living forms, in slumber's play
Oblivious breathe the hours away ;
Like ice-concealed, still-moving streams,
Sleep through your unremembered dreams !

'Hail, mystic Night ! Thy soothing care,
Thy gentle shades, what soul would spare?
Congenial to my mournful moods
Are thy subduing solitudes !'

Thus Mortimer at midnight mused alone,
While the ascending glory of the moon
Streamed through his casement, paling stars,
Fringing th' horizon's distant ebon bars.
⸱ We leave him now; at morn he went his way,
Heaven-guided by religion's fadeless ray.

Another moon had raised its shining head
Above the forest, by bright Venus led ;—
A few calm summer days had glided on
Since pensive Mortimer from home had gone ;—
A thousand locusts beat their winglets thin,
And chirping crickets mingled in the din ;
Insects unnamed their symphonies prolong,
And katy-dids their persevering song ;
The early evening, mild and musical,
Brought peace to all the dwellers of the vale.

'Allie ! Dreaming here alone ?
I have sought you round and round ;
I've a letter for your eye !
Is it worth a pin, or pound ?

'Kiss me, *that* 'tis worth, I know !
It has crossed the ocean far,
As the foreign post-marks show ;—
Sister, dear, how strange you are !

'Never tell us aught about
Lover true across the sea,—

Of a gallant knight away,
  Seeking deeds of chivalry!'

Thus gamboled Helen, but a heart unstrung,
Unprisoned, to her happy sister clung,—
Unburdened hitherto, through sympathy;
Its waves unchided overflowing free,
Grief, startled memory, acknowledged love—
What tides through broken barriers to move!

A page of death—brief tale.   An o'erwrought heart
Waiting and trusting long.   The mortal smart,
Pressure of disappointment, waste of hope;—
In these were powers like those which cope
With nature's sturdiest forms.   In vain the flower
Might gently bend in that o'erwhelming hour:
Love's joy-supporting though sequestered flow
Suppressed as suddenly as one might throw
A shadow o'er a glass; its backward rush
The blossoms on its living borders crush,
Widening, irregular, of destiny
The sport, until subsiding soon, it be
Within itself, o'erspent, waveless, all calm,
Portending, yet so still!   No offered balm
Of kindness now can work its magic there;—
Life totters, apathy succeeds despair.

Oscar was gone.   One stroke of a terrific storm
Mangled in death his noble, manly form;
Amid the Highlands in a summer's day,

With one companion of his pleasure-way,—
One weeping friend to place upon his horse
His master's nerveless, uncommanding curse,
And to his father be its mournful guide;
To turn in mute emotion thence aside
From grief too sudden in its anguish-blow
For any friend's commiseration now,
He went to that mysterious, endless bourn
From whence no traveller's step may e'er return.
  *   *   *   * Thus, 'life is but a span!'
Thus God disposes self-proposing man!'

Recovering slowly from a bed of pain,
The orphan saw the smiling world again;
Awakened from the fever's burning grasp,
She caught the autumn flowerets in her clasp.
  Upon the record of one human breast
'Tis well the cold world's eyes may never rest;
Strange marks are there.   Earthquakes break granite
    rocks
In crevices, with their portending shocks,
Which centuries spread wide but never bind,
And so recurring showers, frost and wind,
Define each angle, curve, and groove, and stain,
For future time's observance; and the train
Of sorrow's forces, pleasure's pang, or thrill
Of joy, deep lines the heart without its will,
When clasping some sweet knowledge as our own,
How breathes the soul in fondness, 'mine alone!'

And when a wound no mortal can allay
Trembles behind reserve, rebuked the ray
That from inquisitive design or art,
Would cheat the secret from the closing heart.

Allien resisted all inquiring thought
Which to unseal love's sacred volume sought;
Gently accepting kind solicitude
Venturing in delicacy, never rude.
Duty becoming her controling rule,
We find her mistress of the village school;—
Spring come again, each morn with blooming cheeks
Its lowly roof, with cheerfulness she seeks.
It stood beside the base of a green hill
Which sloped above the pond and homely mill
Whose rustic, garrulous industry, heard
Far o'er the valley, almost scared the bird,
When undesigning pinions toward it flew;
Whose early morning bell disturbed the dew
By steps industrious, mingling its bright spheres
In shallow streams, as joy sometimes appears.
    A few tall poplars were its pillars green,
A few wild-rose shrubs scattering between;
One apple-tree an orchard had discarded,
Whose yearly fruit was by the urchins guarded,
Marking the northern bound of its arrear,—
These its adornments made the play-ground dear.
But O, how oft the weak, provoking kite,
Failing to soar, in poplar-boughs would light!

How would small fingers stained in June with red,
Oft for the thorn-surrounded roses plead !
How soon May's fairy apple-blossoms sought,
Their falling petals told of ruin brought !
And these were childhood's woes ! They broke no
  rest;
But while their tumults stirred the little breast,
The shadows still were dark, the pangs were deep;
Precursors of those torturers that creep
Insidiously, or boldly, bidding man
Their use and ultimate designs to scan.

A summer day was near its hushing close,
Young zephyrs whispered to the sleeping rose,
A fleecy panoply half veiled the west,
Shading the fainting lily's snowy crest;
The clouds were painted in a hundred dyes,—
Some bore the silver of the noontide skies,
Some caught the fiery sunset's growing flame,
Commingling sapphires for the daylight's wane;
Allien had lingered round her temple long,
And now her voice awakes to joyous song ;
Two happy girls by sweet impulse attend
Her presence, and their artless voices blend
With her pure, free and peace-inspiring strains
That through the air float softly o'er the plains.

   'O, joyously the summer hours
     Are welcoming the night !
   O, tenderly the shrinking flowers

Close in their nectars bright!
And fairies flit through sylvan shade,
In moonlight's silver robes arrayed.

'O, gladly welcome we the time
    When cares distract no more!
Our souls are peaceful as the clime
    Of the Elysian shore,
And gentle raptures thrill the breast,
While nature seeks her holy rest.'

Sinks into silence each soft sound,
While dampness gathers on the ground,
And falling shades more vaguely green,
Render the forest's leafy screen.
    The children clasp their teacher's hands,
Or bend upon the stream's moist sands
To seek in the receding light
Smooth pebbles, mottled, gray or white.
    'Melissa,' youngest of the two,
With curling hair and eyes of blue,
Fearless because her heart so young
No danger knows, no grief has sung,
Has 'neath a shrub's deceptive shade
One step too near the waters made;—
From an unconscious reverie
Allien is startled by one cry,
As if a cherub's voice had lent
Its tone to terror—quickly spent.

One instant,—by the passing tide
She stands, perplexed, o'erwhelmed, defied;
So swiftly has the current wild
Borne from her reach the lovely child!
Long seconds measure her despair,
As far her voice disturbs the air,
Till like the breaking of a dream,
A stranger plunges in the stream!
Suspense—O, terrible its weight!
Till heavy on the broken slate,
The man drew near with burdened arms,
Soothing but deepening love's alarms.
Than all the past this trying hour
Most summons self-possession's power;
To know if that dear life is lost;   '
To comprehend the cruel cost
To one fond mother, young and fair;
To thank the stranger, and to bear
The girl to yonder cottage home;
To pray the living pulse may come,—
All these swift thoughts must be obeyed,
And leaving now the mimic glade,
The full clear moon across their way
Blending pale light with lingering day,
Gives to the features of the child
An angel beauty, heavenly mild.
They're rigid yet, but on her lips
Some warmth is felt; the half-eclipse
Of dull, still eyes—it seems not death,—

There's promise of returning breath.
The stranger and his charge preceding,
Allien the other child is leading ;—
Few words are spoken, short the way,—
Now from the cottage falls a ray
That quickens pace; soon all is told,
And other arms the sufferer hold ;—
Speedy the remedies; the care
Wakes life anew and calms despair.

The stranger bowing from the scene,
His escort offers to Allien
Who, on his courtesy relying,
Refuses not her sweet complying.
    Absorbed in feeling's deepest strength,
Her words are few, until at length
They reach the pastor's humble gate,
Where she, with air considerate,
Bestows new thanks on one unknown,
Almost for saving life o'erthrown!
    Dismissed, the strange recipient
Of gratitude from accident,
With some reluctance turns away;
For on his mind has dawned a ray
Of spirit beauty, new to one
Whose soul is dark, who lives—alone.

Evening's remaining periods closed,
The passive senses all reposed;
Soft slumber's interlacing arms

Clasped round the mind luxurious charms,
Which formed a paradise its own,
Making its hidden music known
To memory, whose failing task
Gave not to morn what morn would ask.
When airy waves of rising day
Far o'er the hill-top spread their way,
The maiden woke, one dream retained,
Which in her reveries long maintained
Remembrance sweet, delightful, clear
As infancy's pellucid tear.
With heavenly purpose, angel-willed,
A mother bent above her child,
Amid a lustrous atmosphere
That brought stellated rays so near,
And made the walls a bloom of light,
She gazed with wondrous new delight
With silvery wings that first unfurled
Their pinions in a sinless world,
And kiss ethereal, she gave
Raptures that e'en forgot the grave.
Her voice breathed notes of song divine;
Her eyes were beauty's smile benign,
And all she whispered of that clime
Unknown to grief and clouds of time,
Made brighter than in days before
The wreaths hope's golden image wore.
But heaven not lingers long below
With sweetest hours the heart may know;

Not long may ecstacies of joy
Resist the gloom of sin's alloy,
And that celestial visitant
Departed, smiling as she went.

Again the solar hour of nine
Rings loud and clear the belfry sign;
The playful urchins hide their balls,
And in the bag the marble falls;
Disjoined are hands, and hushed is song
And o'er the threshold rush the throng;
Across the lintel sunlight streams,
Too slowly marking noonday-beams,
When joyous bounding o'er the meads,
Each step elastic homeward leads;—
A speedy hour, and all return,
Their tedious tasks ere night to learn;
Bending some wistful looks the while
To watch the shades embrace the isle
The river nurses on its breast,
From hills that circle round the west.

Musing perchance on pleasures gone,
The teacher's daily labor done,
Her path pursues along the river
Whereon the feeble sun-lines quiver,
While limpid dews prepare to shine
At morn, on elm and eglantine;
To crystallize each floral crown,
And bind the wings of thistle-down.

A few low words, and by her side
There walks an uninvited guide!
Prompt salutation freely speaks
Some pleasure from her eyes and checks;
No thought has she to countervail
The impress of that evening tale,
How courage, kindness, promptitude,
Rescued Melissa from the flood.
Cherished by feeling, 't was sustained
By all that gratitude defined;—
Not freer noon's unclouded skies
From shade of soul-deformities,—
A deed for memory to embalm
And o'er it sing her gentlest psalm;
And it was now a bond, a tie,
Allien's true heart could not deny;
Causing her impulse kind to swerve
From more habitual reserve,
And, too immediate, the hue
Of admiration's blushes drew
Their rose-waves outward, when delay
Should long have kept them from the day.
 The steps that time her own are grace,
Agility refined ; the face
That bends to mirror her soft eyes,
Sophisticated doubt defies.
'Tis true his orbs are dark and deep,
Where passion's elements may sleep
In subtle designations, seeming

Too like serenity's first dreaming ;
His form is supple, tall, defined
By shoulders not too low, outlined
Like Adonis'; those lips are thin
And rosy; delicate that chin
Is chiseled, sensitive but full ;
Those cheeks in gentle laughter's lull
Have velvet texture, but more pale
Than fair, and sallow more than hale ;
The brow, not high, is white with thought,
The hair with raven shadows frought,
Curls slightly ;—neither young nor old,
His years have not their secrets told ;
And hear his voice—its gentle sound,
Soft, varying, subduing, round
In modulation, trained and sweet,
For artful use was all complete.
It charms directly, unawares,
The inexperienced maiden's ears.

'I paused this morning by the gate
To learn if your sweet childish mate
Had oped her lovely infant eyes
In Earth instead of Paradise !
    By your consent I may express
My sympathizing happiness
That one so beautiful and young
Still lives to share your daily song ;—
Companionship like hers must be

Joy's undisputed ecstacy.'

With checked emotion in her eyes,
Allien to his address replies :
'True.   In my leisure hours the child
Has many saddening thoughts beguiled ;
Her sympathy is fragrance sweet
In many a moment's lone retreat ;
My duties for this partial love,
On lighter pinioned periods move ;
But she restored, so fair, is yet
The author of one vain regret,
The want of power to cancel debt !'

Flashed brighter her companion's eye,—
Self-satisfaction clamored high,
But all concealed its spurring power ;
He stooped and broke a way-side flower,
A purple violet, and prest,
As if with no design, its crest
To briefly silent lips ; enough,—
The tide went back with this rebuff ;
And self possessed, e'en as before
The slightest shade which had spread o'er
His features, cheerily he smiled,
Still speaking of the favorite child ;
We will not call his smile a mask,
Nor of its inward meaning ask.

'Lady, talk not of this to me

Who favored thus first looked on thee;
Who but thy sweet consent would claim
To ask thine own and speak my name;—
The first perchance to me is known,
But I would hear it from thy tone;
And more, fair maiden, wouldst thou tell,
Of all thy beauty lovest well.
A thousand pardons, be there need,
For this request which thou wilt heed!'

'No need but that I here express
My heart's sincerest happiness
To learn the name of one whose arm
Rescued my little friend from harm.'

'Full thanks, sweet maid! who speaks to thee,
A wanderer from all ties free,
No more possessing than his name,
Can but Stelthair de Forest claim;
The Virgin state was once my home,—
Self exiled thence, abroad I roam;
For mother, father, sister, none
Are left to me; and brother, one,
Whose age is mine, whose path unknown.'

Allien bent her averted gaze
Toward the sun's fast mellowing rays,
Which slanted o'er the shrubs and flowers,
The clover-meads and grape-vine bowers,
And lit them for the night retreat

Of insect wings and birdling feet;
Forgetting him who by her side
Walked silent on, her soul's sweet tide
Rippled a few low notes of song,
Which, trembling, half-escaped her tongue,
And bounded thought's deep stillness.
     'Sing,
O, lady, nor restrain one string
Of nature's lute! Earth promised Heaven,
When Music to her care was given,
To grant the child indulgences, to twine
Its form with love; such power is thine!
This favor—one more boon—I ask,—
Surely 'tis no unwilling task!'

'All nature owns the power divine
 Who gave us life and love;—
O see the tranquil glories shine
 In sympathy, above!
The far, adoring, living stars,
 Light-blooming groves of space,
Which twinkling through the cloud's soft bars,
 Make every line a grace!

So let our voices swell in praise
 Let sinless raptures wake
The long-hushed songs of Eden days,
 Our hearts their bliss partake!
Let every spirit grateful own
 Jehovah's sovereign will;
4*

Kneeling recipients of his throne,
   Let every strife be still !

Her strain had ceased, her home regained,
De Forest bowed with air restrained.
Polite and graceful :— 'Sir, good-night,'
And he departed.

          Soft the light
Decreased ; — the summer dreamed
Of many a faded flower redeemed.

And here we pause.   Mirrors of gold
   Wherein another may behold
His fellow's inward life, so fair
   Presenting that no libel there
   May shame offended charity.
   Are rare in God's economy ;
   My feeble muse can claim them not —
   My poor transplanted apricot
Too weak to ask the gardener why
It may not have more rain and sky,
   Dares not expect to draw the vail,
   Disclosing all the serpent's trail ;
   Revealing all love e'en has wrought
In man's perversest gleam of thought ;
   All that philosophy has earned,
   Or passion of its stubble burned —
   All life's experience have proven
   The burdens faith in God hath moven ;
   The germs of good that wake to flower,

In some more pure propitious hour.
But, as through science we behold
Creation's signs — impressions old,
Of buried ages, ere began
The Eden-joy, or sin of man
In coral periods far remote,
When lime-mosaics were afloat
In myriads of living shells
That drank from ocean's briny wells,
Discerning eyes too well may trace
Oft times man's history on his face.

It pleased De Forest well to roam,
Untutored and too soon, from home;
Dangers that threaten all the young,
Denied a mother's counsel tongue,
Beset his path; temptation reaped
Fruits bitterer than wormwood steeped;—
Love's whispers heard but as the call
Of passion's baser carnival,
Pleasure its baleful poppies showering
Where healthful virtues else were flowering,
'Twere not in nature so allied
A problem that its shrine was pride.
Pride not man's crown of dignity,
But weak puerile vanity,
Whose tenderest side is hate of scorn,
Pretext unworthy and forlorn;
But twin-born forms may have no link

Of kindred souls, as though one brink
Of time's vast stream by one was traced
The other on the far shore placed;
So one completed man may be
A contradicted mystery.
Stelthair, what e'er his sins had been
Owned traits of mind too oft unseen;
Which thriving with a heart more pure,
Might joy's companionship secure.
His friendship strong to emulate
High deeds, too selfishly elate
Turned otto to the fumes of gall,
And made their radiance a pall;
Thus estimating acts its own
With commendation's undertone,
Not from a modest but deficient power,
Making its own acceptance cower.
    That he had saved from death a child,
His love of daring flushed and smiled;
That he by this might gain a heart
Already had invoked his art.
Selfish and vain, but not all base,
He in the gentle teacher's face
Saw beauty's confirmation more
Soul-spirited than all before
Of woman's charms that e'er for him
Awoke or sealed deception's dream.
So conquest strengthens when most weak;
So flattery glides like serpents sleek,

When by ignoble minds are sought
Young admiration's wings ; when caught
The impulse wanders, fleet as gold
That flowers the lily's petal-fold.

Where Old Dominion mountains rear
Their brows to meet the tempest's cheer
When rushing from Atlantic's shore,
Sublimely grand their tumults roar,
And break their currents down the hill
To whistle in the valleys shrill ;
To penetrate their cedar shade,
And serenade each flowery glade, —
Where wild Monongahela winds,
And many a green encircling binds,
A rude old house of dingy stone
Afar from hamlet stood alone,
Whose smoky gables frowned forlorn
The day De Forest there was born.
Wild as the region of his birth,
He early longed to roam the earth,
With scarce design, nor purpose grand,
Not love of gain, nor of command,
Nor power to cope with virtue's foe,
None bade him rest, none bade him go ;
Launched on the world's turgescent tide,
Lived not one friend his course to chide.

O, charming sympathetic power,
That makes two hearts to each a flower ;

Whose subtle fragrance moves unseen
Around two souls, but ne'er between!
But flowers are poison now and then—
Beside the daisy in the glen,
Stramonium may rear its cloud
Of dingy green, its trumpet shroud;
A flower that for its deadly freight,
Must abdicate its claim to white.

And sympathy, akin to love ,
So deeply some true hearts may move
They may not see until its strength
Has wandered to a dangerous length,
When, though rebuked, the impulse tells
A mournful tale, like faded shells
That murmur of the treacherous sea,
Loth still to lose its sympathy;
Leading sometimes like love estray,
To thicken griefs along life's way;—
'Tis always well to guard its power,
Nor gather every way-side flower.

Our gentle one embraced the thrill
It brought her heart ; unchiding will
Gave full consent,—from day to day,
Accompanied on her homeward way
By her devoted friend, the vale
Grew shorter by each earnest tale
His rich lips framed,—his step so slow,
So graceful,—she was loth to know
The pathway's end.

'My life's dim day
Is sunned by friendship's holy ray;
O let me wear its beauty long,
And by its favor live more strong;
My heart be its perpetual home;—
I would not bid an orphan roam
The wilds of Earth denied a friend,—
My prayers his footsteps shall attend,
And thus allure my thought from gloom
That binds me to my lost one's tomb;'—
She reasoned thus.
　　　　　　　　One night it came,—
Avowal of the tender flame,
With gentlest play of word and tone,
And softest smile—for her alone;
Eternal vows of constancy;
Asseverations, ecstacy
Of fear and hope,—love's promise fair,
O, was there aught but masking there?

Sweetly she answered, well prepared:—
'I thank you for this kind regard;
But seek to bind no tenderer tie
Than friendship claims, for destiny
Has bound us by no stronger chain,
And this may bring no living pain;—
Accept such pledge ; I can no more;
Love's witchery for me is o'er.'

A shade, a short lip-curl, a frown,

A quick new thought and all were gone;
The artifice was fortified,
And kneeling by the maiden's side,
Where now the grove's more deepening shade
Covert from observation made,
Upraising eyes unused to look
Skyward, again he gently took
Her hand within his own, and sighed,—
O, mimicry of yielding pride!

Resolve was strong, but there was yet
Weakness in sympathy's regret,
Danger for innocence that deemed
The counterfeit the thing it seemed
Allien believed his heart sincere;
Her fancy pictured one bright tear
Trembling upon that manly cheek,—
She tried in vain, she could not speak.
Now list!   A rich harmonious strain
Comes soft, but startling o'er the plain;
The sounds breathe of a living lyre
That personates the soul's desire
And bids its aspirations rise
On wings ethereal to the skies;
Which far from mortal sight can bear
A heart oppressed by sin or care;
Crippled by disappointment's spell;
Wounded because it loves too well;
Wasting because its tender thought

Strives ever, still obtaining nought;
Weeping forever round one shrine,
There always murmuring, '*Mine, O, mine!*'
The world has asked, but who has told
The treasury of music's gold?
Its charms are felt, its power we know,
But where the fount of its full flow?
Poets from suffering learning song,
The ruins of their hearts among;
Lining the down on insect wing;
Inhaling myrrh the while they sing;
Painting the mote of vernal breeze;
Building from leaves of summer trees,
Structures so ornate and so fair
They fall while summer's breath is there;—
These ask of Music where's her home,
And cadences not answers come.
O, be it through the night afar,
Within the paling of some star
That as an angel's diadem
Gives permanence to beauty's dream?—
The human soul becomes its shrine,
Its home and origin divine;—
'Tis all we know, and all we tell
Of Music's overmastering spell.

De Forest and Allien have stood,
Erect and silent by the wood,
Waiting approach of human feet,—

She knows 'tis Helen's voice so sweet
That vibrates on the evening air,
And gives her reassurance there.

'So, I have found you!   Night is near!
Why linger ye so tardy here?'
    A bow from Forest, prompt and low,—
Was't this that flushed her neck of snow?
Not then;—a quick, deep thought had sent
A rose-shade upward; what it meant
Woman can tell.
                    'O, sister, come,
They wait thy presence, dear, at home.'
Her step reversed she led the way,
Singing.   When on the poplars lay
The sun's last golden stripe, alone
The two sat on the door-way's stone;
Helen too gentle to intrude
Upon her sister's silent mood,
Few words were uttered.   One heart gay
With early youth's perpetual May,
The other wearing still the shroud
Of hope, but softened like a cloud
Of silver o'er the morn.

And from that hour she grew reserved,
Watching if friendship still deserved
Her confidence.   She studied well;—
A few brief lessons may dispel   ·
Illusion when a mask discerning,

Truth sets the dry material burning.
'Tis ever difficult to greet,
Acknowledge actions indiscreet;
Their revocation does not smooth
The bitter secret of their ruth;
And while their author writhes within,
Another's hatred may begin;
When to avoid, to him means 'scorn;'
A signal for the demon born
Is compromise of truth or self,
Boldly required by th' clamorous elf.
Allien, in this dilemma, on the plain
One eve her lover met again.
'My love, I came in search of you,
My fond confessions to renew!
Has not your gentle heart repealed
The cruel verdict lately sealed?
You truly love me :—Answer, yes;—
Let those sweet lips the truth confess!
Allien, be mistress of my bower,
Its bright exotic, queenly flower;—
Let no barbarian tendrils dare
Embrace my rose, my treasure rare!
Sit down upon this velvet grass
And bless the breezes as they pass!
O, come, my love, my darling, come,—
No more from your adorer roam!'

Surprised, she yet found quick reply,

And raised her frank reproving eye,
Resting on his, till inward born,
They shot their burning rays of scorn;
Decrees of conscious dignity
Commanding deference instantly.

Peace brooded o'er the quiet world;
Blue smoke-wreaths o'er the hamlet curled;
Around it wound the river slow,—
Anon the winds begin to blow;
The sinking sun far in the west,
Behind a cloud conceals his crest;
And darkly up a sombre vail
Spreads o'er the sky its troubled sail;—
Now hoarse, low thunders break, and tell
The August day's disturbed farewell;—
Blue lightnings flashing here and there,
Foretell a fearful storm is near.
Allien before her window bends,
Musing on life and worthless friends;—
Memory and love too intertwining,
One last sad scene is grief defining,
Transporting her in swift caprice,
O'er many a league of watery space;
She greets broad moors and mountains grand,
The dowry of a rugged land;
Walking alone o'er mossy braes,
Where Oscar roved in other days,
Reflection pained still, asking 'why,'

Eternal echo its reply.
O, images of lost delight,
Life's multiplying parasite,
Feeding on hope that else might bloom,
Your conquests all too quickly come!
How scarce the mind regards the lie
Of opulent air-buildings! Fie!
Then what is all reality
But broken strata, grief and joy,
The gold less weighty than alloy!

But where is Stelthair Forest now?
Maturing a revengeful vow:—
'Shall I endure her maiden scorn?
Was I to such dishonor born?
She yet must feel that man has power
To crush as well as love a flower!'

Pacing a closely shuttered room,
Unmindful of the storm and gloom,
Of night, or nature's stern demands,
Describing circles with his hands,—
Ignoring sleep, forgetting food,—
That fiendish passion, thirst for blood,
Possessed his being, nerve and soul,
Assuming absolute control.
Again he speaks:—'My certain aim
Shall quench the life, put out the flame,
And not imploring eyes shall quail
My nerve, or make my purpose fail;

Then, honor ! thou art bright as now ; —
Stelthair recants no vengeful vow !

A score of hours on dull wings flown,
Another gentle day has gone,
A play fatigued and guileless lamb
Lies down at night beside its dam,
Upon the fragrant turf to rest.
Unthinking what has veiled the crest
Of noon's glad sun ; so softly slept
Allien, who long erewhile had wept,
Till prayer and wearied nature soothed
Her mind to seek its dreaming food ;
She slumbers ; o'er her swelling breast
The moonbeams steal to give attest
To fairer beauty on her brow,
And make the shadows wonder how
The lillies left the night parterre,
To smile in sweet contentment there !
Quiet as airs before a storm
She dreams of no impending harm ; —
Sweet odors through the casement stealing
'Mid listless vines around it wreathing,
Bear no low periods of sound ;
Bright burns the stars by space embound ;
Reposes all the garden bloom,
Silence and rest are in the home,
    She starts, — one snowy hand is o'er
Her scattered tresses flung, before

Her sleeping eyes the other prest
In momentary half unrest,
And all again is calm and still
As icy chains can bind a rill.

The vines are torn aside ; he creeps
Adroitly, then he noiseless leaps,
And by the spotless shrine he stands,—
What stream shall cleanse his murderous hands ?
O, base, deceived, misguided man !
No mortal eye has power to scan
The dark confusion of thy heart,
Where pale remorse may fix its dart
Of poison,—burning, deadly strife,—
And phantoms round thee sway the knife
Whence ever-falling drops.of blood
Whisper, 'from innocence we flowed !'
Thy tortured soul's self-kindled fire
May not consume its new desire,
But murder's living, clamorous stain
There seek its duplicate to gain.
Earth's beauty,—moonbeams, stars and flowers,
Be thy reproach for future hours ;—
In the open dungeon of thy mind,
Still chained, thy hopes shall be confined.

He dares disturb her angel dreams,
And smothering all her rising screams,
Bears swift away her fainting form
By strength derived from passion's storm

Of red revenge, whose gloating eye
Is feasting on its easy prey.

    Passing the lawn, beyond the well,
The garden where great shadows fell
From hoary elms that frowned more stern
As seemed their boughs the crime to learn,
He laid his burden down beside
The river's noiseless limpid tide,
Before his lovely victim stood,
The shame of calm night's solitude.

Reviving now, escaping fear,—
Serenity's death-harbinger,—
Raising her full, clear eyes on him,
Looking a star that nought might dim,
A light of truth-pledged destiny,—
A dove from love's eternity ;—
So mute and calm before her fate,—
Where creeps the relish of his hate?
She speaks : 'Stelthair, may God forgive your sin
Jesus your soul from darkness win.
I've not *deceived* you ; 'tis your own
Proud heart that wrongs, not me alone,
But wastes your peace ; I've been your friend,
But have no power to comprehend
That *love* in such disguise can seek
To take false vengeance on the weak.'

In vain, in vain ! Given o'er, enslaved
By passion's minions, thoughts that raved

'Neath brambling conscience ; maddened will
Rushed, fire-impelled, demoniac still :—
Chimera, controversion, doubt,
When peace sleeps o'er her resting lute,
And man looks god-like, wanting God's
Foreknowledge of the guilty loads
He then so calm, must yet bear on,—
Life's sad inheritance to man !

To give the one decisive hlow
Stelthair's right arm is lifted slow,
As if some pure compulsive eyes
Restrained him from yon starry skies !
But hate impels the weapon's course,—
Alas ! it speeds with cruel force,
Her suffering heart sends forth its wail,
The moon-rays pale confess the tale,
The dark empurpling stains that spread
Upon her snowy dress * * * Dead?
Life's stream arrested in its tide
To gratify revenge and pride ?

' 'Tis done,' half andibly he cries,
And stoops to close her nerveless eyes ;
O, has not pity's faithful thought
One sigh for ruin grossly wrought,
One deep, redeeming impulse then
To mourn, and ask the hour again ?
Can human hearts where love resides
Resign to deeds that shame derides

5   G

Their whole domain ?　Ah me, the sin
A tampering soul may nurse within
Till all the court be darkness !

　　　　　　　　　　Done,
'Twas next to flee.　Remorseful one,
What refuge shall efface thy deed !
What subterfuge declare thee freed
From thy corroding, self-bound chain,—
What antidote relieve thy pain ?
　Plunging in deepest shade, he flies
Engulfed in night's black mysteries
A surer victim than the one
Mistaken love could so disown !

Life's spark was not entirely gone ;
The tottering brain resumed its throne ;
The sluggish heart began to feel
The baffled effort of the steel ;
As on the hard and dew-cold sand,
While night wore on in silence grand ·
And stars up toward the zenith drew ;
Allien still lay alone ; she knew
The arm of God had fettered back
Destruction's arrow in her track,
That morn and safety were before her,
Truly as angels watching o'er her.

Rejoicing in the sunny morn,
Her sister's tresses to adorn,
Bright Helen seeks her, wondering why

Allien sleeps 'neath such brilliant sky !
Glad notes are trilling from her tongue,—
The yielding door is open flung,—
Lo ! where is Allie ?   None have yet
Her morning salutation met !
And seeing there her daily dress,
Her features change to doubt's distress,
While flying from the rifled room
To give the house the strange alarm.
And forth it went like light and sound
So quickly, all the village round ;
While all the household run to seek
Some signs within the grounds to speak
The dear one's fate ; no thought have they
Consent allowed her steps to stray :
Some violence has borne her from
The shelter of her second home !

Lost !   'Tis a word that claims the tomb
For company, love's tone of doom,—.
Sometimes it trifles ; then it kills
Grand hopes and lovely : 'tis like mills
To millions of gold sovereigns, yet
Its meaning mourners ne'er forget.
Something is found when joy is lost—
'Tis misery.   When death has crost
Our threshold twice, something is left
Not there before : bosoms bereft
May keep the shadows, hoping still ;

But *lost!* explaining not the ill
Befallen one we love, to hear
Is but the climax of despair.

Allien is found, and on the crowd
Of anxious ones around her bower,
While on a softer couch she lies,
She looks with weak and wondering eyes
As though forgotten were the hour
She 'scaped the murderer's deathly power.
But nature sank beneath the shock,
And wasting fever seemed to mock,
Week after week, all efforts made
To save the sufferer from the dead :
Then, feeling little sense of pain,
Her thoughts in lethargy remain,
Till with a dirge like interposing
The windy Autumn's wail is closing '
The dying glory of the year,
When chillier shadows reappear,
And shriller through the rifled bowers
Stern prophecies of Winter hours
Rebound up the bracing air,
While dead leaves flutter here and there,
And mouse and squirrel stow away
Sweet nuts to cheer the Wintry day.
Attended with the tenderest care,
Her spirit then awakes to share
In fond affection's certain light

The pastimes of the frosty night.
Once more did hope inspire her way,
Giving contentment with its ray,
So like these hidden streams that sleep
In desert sands, but e'en more deep,
One name and episode were gone,
To feeling and to thoughts unknown.

The bridal bells are pealing !
A bridal vow is sealing !
    A maiden by the altar stands ;
The crown of snow-drops on her hair
Is rivaling her neck so fair,
    And proudly holds her fairy hands
A noble youth of burning eye,
Whose brow of thought is arched and high ;
    And while a breath of air can stir
The drapery that decks his bride—
A gossamer aerial tide—
    He stands as though a worshiper
And see ! the throng that round them wait
With admiration are elate,
    And many a beauty envies more
    The peerless Helen than before !

Such words as angels love to hear
Are breathed while flows affection's tear ;
    And hope embodied seems to tell
Of bright advancing years of joy,
Of streams of bliss with no alloy,

Proceeding from the heart's deep well
Now tender salutations greet
The wedded pair ;—on feathery feet
    The soft approving moments hie ;—
Parental hope, parental pride,
Close pensive round the happy bride,
    And like Arcturus in the sky,
Eclipsing *reulluras** far
Shines Helen the acknowledged star !

Now mirth and festive gladness
Divert all thought of sadness :
    Sweet, gay, melodious songs are heard ;
Rich cadences the young and fair
Wake on the bright perfumed air
    Ring, rivaling the forest bird!
The early hours of evening seem
The melting visions of a dream,
    Till in the outward stillness, loud
    The midnight's chime is sent abroad.

The scene has passed, forever passed ;
Too joyous and too pure to last !
    The wedding night has left its seal
Upon the elastic heart—no change
Can break, no gloom estrange ;
    Eternity may e'en reveal
The gentle shimmerings of its light,

---

* Reullura, in Gaelic, means beautiful star.—THOMAS CAMPBELL.

Far in the gloam of mortal night.

Once more sweet Spring is on the plain,
With birds and blossoms in its train:
Once more the sea-green spires of grass
Bend softly as the breezes pass.
Unprisoned brooks in wider bound
Are threading silver o'er the ground,
And Robin-red-breast, shy and free,
Has sought the loftiest cherry-tree,
The shadiest bough, to build a nest
Where five blue eggs awhile will rest;
And when the luscious fruit is ripe,
Gleaming with red and amber stripe,
The nest will stir with tiny life,
As rosy mouths in twittering strife
Open to catch the morsel dear
The parent drops from branchlet near.

O, happy birdlings, ye were made
Sad hearts from weeping to dissuade;
Muses of Spring, of wood, and height,
Where proud the eagle plumes his flight;—
Ye guardians of the blossoms fair!
Ye living blisses of the air!

The child of love's baptismal vow,
Breathing in pure religion's flow,
From life's first morn, through all her days,
Our orphan loved the Lord. Truth's rays

From love's eternal fountain shone
On her young soul; when most alone
'T was time's perpetual eloquence,
Celestial hope's munificence.
But 't was this last dark stroke that brought
Clearer conviction to her thought;
And duty's outward form became
Confession of the Savior's name.

O, could we draw aside the screen
This and another world between,
And view with tireless mortal eyes
Yon bright celestial Paradise
Where arms are wings, where sound is song,
And robed in light are the vast throng
Of blissful beings who fulfill
Untempted the Creator's will;
Where never more the heart may yearn
Unsatiate for love eterne;
Where soul-companionship complete
Makes every thought one thrill more sweet
Than years of ecstacies may prove,—
Earth-mingled, ever-changing love—
O, not to draw the glory down,
But purer grow to look upon
Beauty and joy to sin unknown!

Sweet and serene the Sabbath-smile,
While softly up the narrow aisle
Allien advances, now to kneel.

In humbleness her heart must feel,
Before the simple altar ; there
Her foster father stands in prayer;
He reads the vows of covenant,
And then the holy sacrament
Is first partaken.   In Heaven above
Glad angels feel new thrills of love,
And stronger goes the pilgrim forth
To tread the thorny ways of Earth.

Advancing toward the western hills,
Above the river and its rills,
Upon the outskirts of Glendale,
There lies a deep and narrow vale,
Or wooded glade ; 'tis rarely sought,
Save by the lone and sad in thought:
Perchance the aged man may seek
At eventide, with visage meek,
The ancient shades to muse upon
Years of full pleasure long since gone ;—
Lovers sometimes there, arm in arm,
Walk almost mute with love's new charm;
There now and then the school-boy's feet
Rove, not so near, and soon retreat.
     It has been said, when night's dark mail
Conceals the glade, a broken wail,
As of a spirit's brief return,
From o'er the hill-top sounding, worn,
Monotonous and deep and weird,
     5*

Trembling anon, as if a tired
And aged voice discoursed in vain
Resemblance of its youthful strain,
Has oft been heard ; but while the ear
Bends yet reluctantly to hear,
A sudden silence may succeed,
And then a light the vision lead
Increasing as it settles down
Upon the tallest tree's dark crown ;
Growing more lurid in its flame,
Till, as you gaze, a mystic name,
Or word, is lettered boldly there,—
A moment and 'tis lost in air !

Superstition !   Child of Fear and Night ;
Sister of Ignorance and Blight ;
Arrayed in cloud, sustained by gloom,
Rejecting all that might illume,
Thou art a shadow, else a fire
Within a rock, or blank desire
For what thou never canst attain,—
A fire-fly on a marshy plain
Emitting one faint, failing gleam
Beneath a star's eternal beam !

'T was said, these moans were from a mound,
The green high centre of the ground
Between the knoll and hill, whereon
No trees had grown through ages gone,
Nature disclaims her impress there,

And art will scarce the symbol bear;
'T was fashioned by an absent race,
And was the Indian's burial place.
The spectral radiance came from far,
Memento of extinguished war;
And STOCKBRIDGE was the fiery name
Outlined amid this midnight flame.

Behold a scene that knew the past,
From whence tradition's shadows cast
Vague records. 'Tis a mortal scene,
Of life and death of what has been!
    Tall forms, athlete and sinewy, move
In dark procession through this grove;
Erect each head, each lip comprest,
Solemn and slow each naked breast
Swells high in speechless grief profound,—
The red-brown brows with plumes are crowned;
The eyes indulge a vacant gaze;
The hands bear stalks of ripening maize,
And wampum wealth, to lay beside
The warrior in his deathly pride;
He died not in the strife of war,
And o'er the mystic river far,
Plying in silence his dark oar,
By these sustained, he wants no more.
    So when perchance a dark-eyed maid
Is for her narrow home arrayed,
They bear white wreaths of thorn-flowers woven

To crown her for the Indian's Heaven.
　　The nerveless form aloft is borne
Speaking, though still, to those who mourn,
As deeply if acutely less
Than Saxon hearts in such distress:
'Tis half-erect, robed as in life;
The tomahawk — at rest from strife —
Lies by the corse, his eagle-plume
Is painted gaily for the tomb.

Now years have gone, and so have they;
Descendants of the Stockbridge stray
On distant prairies rich and broad,
With wider canopy o'erhead,
But less of forest, more of plain,
And vaster streams that to the main
Bear yearly tide.
　　　　　　　In Summer nights
Made pensive by the starry lights,
The aged warriors sigh to roam
The precincts of their fathers' home,
To bathe in Housatonic's waves,
And build again around their graves
The tribute fires.   So with each year
When days of Summer disappear,
Some scattered lodges there bespeak
Return; but what the pilgrims seek
Seems unexplained, all more than this,—
Strange children of the wilderness!

They scarce disturb the squirrel's home,
So silent is the Indian's gloom ;
Around the huts the peaceful ones
Move, speaking but in monotones,
And reverently tread the ground
Of that lone cemetery's bound ;
Pointing below, and then above,
Like those who know a Savior's love.

Beneath the young leaves' quivering shade
Allien roves often to this glade
For pale anemones in Spring,
Or richer blooms the Summers bring ;—
In Autumn, too, when beech and oak
Are crimsoned darker in the smoke
Of fires re-kindled, oft she makes
Her way through interlacing brakes,
And thickets wild, and gazes on
The burial-mounds of warriors gone.
She ponders on the mournful fate
Of people rude, but strong and great;
The primal owners of the soil,
But chary of husbandric toil ;
Unlettered, stern and unrefined,
Unpolished both in mien and mind;
Unknown to geographic sweep
Of rock or plain, or waters deep,
Or measure of the Earth ; the wild
Free, bold, courageous, athlete child

Of forest shades, and water-cove,—
Offspring of Heaven's omniscient love.

Pride, sentinel of classic walls,
Watcher of old baronial halls,
Safe-guard of beauty, shield of flowers,
Spirit of antique arms and powers ;
Thine upward glance and diamond eye,
Soaring as eagles clouds defy,
Or gathering ruins' fragments grand
To build again with unseen hand ;
Restoring base and column vast,
And capital and cornice, cast
In Gothic or Ionian mould,
Entablature and friezes old,
With pediment and architrave,
From dim oblivion's open grave,—
Thou know'st as well the red-man's breast
As the Circassian emperor's crest !
    And Strength, the nations' wand of power,
Is too his natural boast and dower ;—
Treasure and danger of many lands,
God-woven in its cordon bands,
Olympiac triumph, Helvic boast,
Teutonic crown, Caledonia's cost,—
This the supplanted Indian keeps
Within his soul as thunder sleeps.
    And courage, thou sustainer grand
Of human reason, sight and hand ;

Thou art for him a legacy
Of all mankind's fraternity!

The blue-bells of New England rung
A fairy cadence as they hung
Suspended by their threads between
Dark spreading boughs of evergreen,
O'er-hanging rocky precipice
Where time has left its hoary kiss,
And storms have beat and washed in vain
To eradicate the Bluebeard-stain.
Their music herald was of June,
When Nature's harp in highest tune,
Inspired the soul's responsive lyre
To send its grateful music higher.
  Before she bids a last adieu
To all the scenes her childhood knew,
The orphan goes one evening forth
To moisten with her tears the earth
Where what remains in ashes rest,
Of forms loved earliest and best.
Beside her parents' graves she kneels,
And inexpressive sadness feels
As thought   uncurbed, with eager wing
Speeds back to life's more early Spring,
Bearing a chastened, solemn trace
Of that most consecrated place.
The rippling of a Lethean stream
Is holy in the passing dream:

Though weeping-willows o'er it bear
The beauty of the past is there—
Her sacred past,—and by its brink
The same bright daisies love to drink:
There Summer cloudlets—fairy isles—
As long ago, seem Heavenly smiles :—
O, hallowed scene! O, brief return!
Your feeble lights so softly burn!
   These spirits of her infant home
Almost dispel her wish to roam
Afar where danger marks the track,
For oh! her childhood has come back.—
—'Tis gone! The freshening of the breeze
Wakes mournful sounds among the trees;
And fitful beats the pulse of day,
As changing more the shadows gray
Of shrub and tree become more dense,
More gloomy to the o'erwrought sense.
From yonder wood she hears the owl,
Dolorous, while a cloudy cowl
Conceals the recess of the west,
And birdling throats grow still in rest.
   So silent all, so lone and sad,
Shrinks not that youthful heart in dread
Of night's weird marshaling of powers
Known but to darkness,—phantom hours,
Time's wandering ministers that bring
Decrees from some Plutonian king?
Of nature's mysteries no fear,

Of white-vailed ghostly tenanter
Of grave-yards ; shrieks, and sighs, and moans
That bear no like to human tones?
Ah, na Not one condemning page
Of superstition, pretence sage,
Trembling imposter, truth's disguise,
Has ever fed her spirit eyes.
So, still she lingers kneeling there
Her white dress waving in the air,
Like a banner from etherial spheres,
Love-calling o'er the vale of tears.

Bounded by shadows deepening more,
A slow-descending, light-winged shower
Encircles the lonely votary
As if to bear her far away,
And woo her to a sweet forgetting
Of sorrow's mute perpetual fretting.

Her senses more entranced, she hears
Music too soft for mortal ears,
And, too, a slight electric stir
Of wings. A heavenly visitor
Salutes her there : their sympathy
Complete, as when from eye to eye
Love meets its own ecstatic ray,
Asking but it love's debt to pay.
A voice—familiar ? No, not now,
But O, so tender long ago !
Such words are whispered,—'Heaven is love !
We watch and wait thy steps above !'

'My mother,' dies upon her lips,—
Those mortal eyes are in eclipse:
No cloud, no solitude, alone
No more; the day cannot be gone!
O yes, 'tis gone. The solemn night,
Its full dominion holds: the light
Of clouded stars burns not below,
The atmosphere repels it so.

Spirits feel not the weight of time
But as a bell by its own chime
Vibrates when sound has ceased. Allien
Was like a disembodied one,
And there until the morning's dawn
Gave token that the screen was drawn
Homeward to night, beside the tomb
She still reclined; an ostrich plume
Than she no fairer, no more pure;
But something longer to endure,
Trembles her form, and blends this strife
Of perishing and fadeless life.

Awaking with a feverish start,
As if her sweet and gentle heart
Were pierced by th' soft but arrowy light,
The vague remembrance of the night,
And her bath of dew so bright and chill,
Sends through her frame a shivering thrill,
A brief bewilderment of fear;
Asking, 'why do I linger here?'

She rises on her numb cold feet,
And hastens from the lone retreat.
Again at home, inquiring eyes
And words, meet kind reserved replies,
Believing, as the night before,
She stayed within a dear friend's door;—
Vailing the tumult of her breast,
She bars her room for needed rest;—
Benignant nature gave it soon,—
She slept till day was high in noon.

*   *   *   *   *   *

'"The way is long," the father said,
As through the Western wilds he sped
   With eager searching eye;'—
An emigrant with courage bold
Who has no thought for paltry gold,
   Conducts a numerous family
To find a home of sweet content
   Where quiet years may yet be spent.

Allien,— an angel in the band,—
Still ponders on her native land,
   But no regretting tears arise;—
The courage of the Christian heart
Can foil the tempter's secret dart;—
   She gazes on the evening skies
As sets each day o'er plain or stream
The Summer sun's warm guiding beam.

Her consecrated thoughts delight
To watch its daily promise light;—
    She soothes the matron's anxious fear,
While heavenly grace, like timely showers
Refreshes all her life-sweet powers;
    And in the distance rays appear,
Diffusing from Religion's lamp
Around the red-man's sombre camp.

———

Now close the curtain—bind it well,—
Let no intrusive glimpses tell
The sequel of the far away
Wherein our noble one shall stray.
    Time, though so absolute and stern,
Enable fancy to discern
The record Mississippi's wave
Has murmured for an orphan's grave

PART SECOND.

Awake, my harp, in silence lain,
Sing wilder the concluding strain;
But human life and love still be
Thy light, thy theme, thy minstrelsy!
Though sometimes wrung from seas of grief,
Let every word, and line, and leaf,
Bear witness of the heart's deep truth,—
Of nature and the strength of youth!
   May Helicon consent to give
The flow of song for which I live;
To smile in Heaven-reflecting streams,
And chain the witchery of dreams!
   Fair Faith! Indulgent Hope! O, stand
To guide my trembling, tracing hand,
When visions of repelling storms
Assail my thought's embodying forms!
   Sweet Muse, forsake me not, but lend
Thy harp, with mine, though weak, to blend
Poetic harmonies of soul,—
Blest Goddess, all my notes control!

Beyond a faintly shimmering stream
The Indian hunters' watch-fires gleam,
  Soft shine night's early stars;
The air is stirred by unseen hands,
Dim phantoms wander forth in bands,
  The ghosts of Indian wars;
Of conflicts long ago maintained,
When vengeance, battling unrestrained,
  Laid many a warrior low;
When fierce, exultant yells broke forth,
Which quailed the Spirit of the North,
  Whose rains were turned to snow.

A band have paused the stream beside,
The haze is darkening o'er the tide,
Shrouding the bluffs and sweeping plains
Where solitude has loosed its chains,
  And woods have circled back,
Since steam disturbed the wild-cat's play,
And dawned improvement's waking ray
  Far o'er this Western track;—
Courage and hope have struggled long,
And love revives a fervent song
Of pleasures past the heart has urned
Since youth to manhood's courses turned,
  Forgetting childhood's dreams;—
Bright flames arise between the boughs,—
The perfect moon but half allows
  Its early evening beams;—

Our travelers pitch their lonely tent,—
A prayer devout to Heaven is sent,
   And wearied forms repose ;
Children, and sire, and matron fair,
And she who claims their guiding care,
   Glendale's transplanted rose.

The tide that flows between the camps,
Silvered by moon and starry lamps,
   Majestic sweep its lines ;
From snows perpetual—far away—
Where hardy trappers rarely stray,
   And frost has dwarfed the pines,
To ever-blooming tropic groves
Where man, the friend of nature, roves,
   With love of ease increast ;
Where fruits perennial blush to lure
The eye and hand, as when the pure
   First parents spread their feast.

FATHER OF WAVES. The mightiest stream
That ever caught a starry gleam !
Behold his countless curves of grace,—
With one vast gaze of thought, O trace
   His stateliness of tide,
The numbering thousands of his miles,
The grand remoteness of his isles,
From rippling source to yonder sweep,
Where mingling with the ocean deep,
   He claims it for his bride !

The morning sunbeams' purple light
Pursues the wavering shadows' flight,
   Disseminating day ;—
Alas ! that heart-shades linger still,—
That life may be a woodland rill,
   Meeting no sunny ray
Until far wandering o'er the plain
It may escape the forest train,
   And bound with new delight !
Patient, Allien !   Though clouded now,
Thy path grows dim, though stern thy vow,
   Trust God for future light.

With solemn hearts but not forlorn,
The wanderers awake at morn,—
A raft e'er noontide bears them o'er
The river to the western shore ;—
A few days progress, and beside
Missouri's rival tribute tide
Their journey ends.   Possession marks
Their home ; ax-riven barks
Of skirting trees give legal bounds
To their uncultivated grounds.
No time is lost, an open space,
A gentle slope, is th' chosen place,
The well-selected, sunny spot,
Where logs soon form a sheltering cot.

From that day forth a hamlet spread,
As emigrants were thither led ;

And though the Indians' camp-fires gleamed
Around it, and the panther screamed
At night, and muskets primed for fire
Were grasped by brother, son or sire,
Peace blessed the region far and near,
And patient toil dismembered fear.

A missionary years before
Had left Atlantic's distant shore,
By Heaven directed through the wild
To bless the heathen forest-child.
Allien her resolution made
To seek this Christian brother's aid
Escorted by her guardian's son,
The last long mile one evening won,
Their steeds pause by a cabin, near
A lovely lake, whose surface clear,
Embalm the boughs that o'er it bend,
And for its watery kiss contend.
    The air is still; no ruffling breeze
Sends quivering sunlight through the trees;
No woodland whisper, soft and slow,
Disturbs reflections dark below;
The leafy-pictured masses sleep
Like tired explorer's of the deep.

A breath, a ripple on the tide !—
A birch canoe with silent glide
Darts forward,—eagle plumes appear,—
A warrior in his proudest gear.

Bounds on the sloping weedy shore;
His bark secured, he strides before
The cot, sits down upon the grass,
Shaded by boughs of sassafras.

Meanwhile the inmates gather near
The strangers' names or tale to hear;—
Their looks and manners well confest
The new surprise of every breast.
  The missionary round whose brow
The locks of youth were turned to snow
With kind, inquiring, gentle mein,
Imparted courage to Allien.

'Kind sir, my errand soon is told,—
An orphan girl in me behold,
Who from a pilgrim valley come,
Would teach the Indian in his home:
Not friendless or alone I traced
The leagues between with hope and zest;
My guides were true and loving souls;—
Not far away their cot;—where rolls
Missouri from the sunset, we
Now dwell; a simple coterie:
Some moons have waned since there they chose
The spot whereon the cabin rose;
And you, kind sir, will not refuse
The strength approval may infuse?
Behold me ready for the task,—
Jesus will give the grace I ask.'

'Welcome, fair daughter of the East,
And more, if duty be thy quest!
Thy form is frail, and young thy heart,
To bear the missionary's part ;
But storms may leave unhurt the reed,
When mighty oaks must break and bleed ;—
According to thy strength thy day,—
The soul has power that loves to pray.'

Trembling the plumes above his brow,
The listening Indian rises now ;
A deep unyielding fervor lies
Behind the sable of his eyes ;—
As from their coral halls may creep
The subdued waters cf the deep
To marshal mountain waves in storm,
So full, expansive grows his form ;
Speaking, not as the tempest sounds—
Not as the echo far rebounds—
Yet grandly as the sea-tides swell
When night-winds bid the day farewell.

'The Christian's Manito is mine. His light
Broke through my dark, dark heart, and gave it love !
The red-man's thought is proud—his eyes are blind—
His pride shall fall. A clouds are scattered from
The prairies shall his eyelids be unbound !—
God sent the maiden. Far across the streams
Whose waters laugh in Spring-time—far beyond
The cloudy hill-tops—many moons away —

A few brave warriors trode the distance back
To hunting-grounds once rich—deserted. There,
Beside our own blue stream, we sat us down
To sigh—to view the past. This tender bird
Poured out such strains as sing the pines at night
When hunters rest. She wandered through the groves,
And once—the last—*I saw a pale face dare*
Lift his weak arm to slay the singing bird
Of Housatonic! Paler grew the moonlight—
It withered on the boughs—the midnight's breath
Was angry—I sprang forth. His guilty path
I followed. In the deep, dark woods I broke
His way. The black and bloody stain—the crime
Great Manito—the Christian Manito
Forbids; the crime he curses, there was marked
Upon his coward brow. Then I avenged
The helpless one. I brought him low. Before
That moon grew dark our steps had traveled toward
Our sunset home! Now has she flown
Back o'er the stream of death, to cheer and bless
My race! The power of Manito is here!
She comes like sunbeams round a chasm dark,
To tell the chiefs there's death and sorrow near!'

Ah! Retribution! Come it will
For every wrong we may fulfill,
In this life or another. Sin
May backward hurl its javelin
And punish in the mortal, or

Its later penalty is sure:
Ages change not the least design
Of law or government divine.
  Stelthair, we pity thy sad fate
But no recall comes by regret;
Commiseration, sympathy,
Heals not the spirit's leprosy:
We would have warned thee—what avail!
Encased within thy pride's dark mail,
O, what to thee remonstrance then,
Thy deadly purpose was so plain!
O, didst thou not relent, and feel
The pain redemption's plan may heal?
Too late, alas! to save thy life
From the assassin's secret knife,
Who, instrument of Heaven, thought,
Avenging innocence, he ought
Destroy thee thus!

Emotions words have ne'er exprest
O'ercome Allien, and rack her breast;
Her bowing head is overwrought
With deep but yet tumultuous thought,
While memory's restoring power
Concenters on that awful hour:—
The present lost like lightning flames,
The past returns with all its aims;
Life's shattered hopes are broken chains,—
Each link dissevered still remains

Scattered around her pensive feet,
Pale ruins of her love's defeat.

Aroused to duty's present call,
She breaks the spell, escapes the thrall,
And draws each listener round her near,
For all her simple words would hear.

'No time is this for grief and sighs;
From sad remembrances I rise,
To spend my time and strength for those
To whom I may some truth disclose.
That hour is gone:—My name, Allien;
I've wandered to this forest green,
An alien's child;—my father—he
Sought exile in a land more free;
Crossing the ocean in his youth,
For love and liberty—sad ruth!—
He lives, and my sweet mother, where
The angels breathe in sinless air.'

Another morn illumes the Earth;
A thousand things of life have birth;
Wild music echoes through the wood,
And ripples soft the lake's mild flood.
Before the sun had tinged the trees
With beauty's gold auxiliaries,
When rest made sleep no longer ease,
And sweetly cooed the mated dove,
And red-birds piped their notes of love;
When whip-poor-wills and owls of night

Were coverted from morning light,
Allien and her young escort stood
Prepared again to trace the wood.
Reining their steeds, the last word said,
They took the path that homeward led,
And 'neath the shadowing branches sped .
Oh ! moral courage nerved her breast
And gave her lonely journey zest,
Strengthening a pure heroic mind,
To bless and benefit her kind.

Dim, low and small, a shelter rude
From wind or rain, a temple crude,
Upon a slope from whose earth-breast
A hundred oaks have broke the rest
Of germs invisible and brief,
To show their heraldry of leaf,
And grow in power from year to year,—
Before a lakelet deep and clear,
A bark-thatched hut in fancy seen,
Discloses where the kind Allien
Draws from her energies each day,
Teaching the young to read and pray.
They 're Indian children, but they feel,
And love their instincts will reveal.
There 's look inquiring in the eye,
There 's meaning smile and motion shy ;
They watch the intermingling flow
Of word and kindness :—as God's bow

Divides the cloud, disparting so,
By beauty's agency, new light
From darkness ; they grow bright
In love's defining medium,
Set 'tween their native night and them;
These infant scions of the wood,
Of fathers in whose veins the blood
Of mystic lineage dilates,
Ignoring all historic dates.
And in those breasts are warm desires,
Though latent as volcanic fires
When long suppressed the flowers may bloom
On the crater's edge as on a tomb.

Patient she labors, day by day,
And studies by the taper's ray
The few brief phrases that convey
Her meanings to the little band
Who seem to love her soft command.
She seeks by symbol rude and sign
To fix attention, to combine
With irksome study, pleasure's cheer,
While each dark face becomes more dear,
And eyes flash forth their new delight
As kindly instincts shine more bright,
And love rejoicing in its own
Has warm and more responsive grown.
 Each dusky urchin vies to bring
The captured bird of brightest wing,

The snowy egg, the eagle's nest,
Rare blossoms from the bluff's high crest,
The pebble bright and tinted shell,
And mosses from the cedar dell;
Treasures of all those vast domains
Whose loss the Indian disdains.

She taught the Sachem's favorite son,
Whose turbulence was gently won
By her inexplicable power,
As though a thorn might ope to flower!
Too young to string the warrior's bow,
The chief allowed the prince to go,—
To roam alone the unfenced wild,
To climb the ledge by ages piled,
And gaze upon the surging tide
That laved its base, in boyish pride.
　　Owasso found the teacher's cot,
And henceforth daily sought the spot;
As wings the eaglet toward the sky,
Yearning his new-found powers to try,
His strong, untutored soul awoke
When to his comprehension spoke
Some gleams of beauty more refined,
A wider sweep of heart and mind,
And struggling germs of intellect,
Of feeling's ken and self-respect,
Expanding, answered wisdom's call
From nature's rule tyrannical.
　　6*　　　　I

So wild, and unrebuked, and free,
Too boisterous for sincerity,
Owasso now from day to day
Became more gentle in his play.

Believest thou the Indian heart
With all its innate cruel art,—
Revenge that rests like sheath-hid steel,
No warming gratitude may feel?
When love, or pride, or peace are full,
The mind not always marks the lull
Or period brief which then divides
Bright paths from overwhelming tides :—
Danger stalks near with lurid brow,
Arrayed in guise of light, the glow
Accepted as propitious powers,—
The heart oft weakest when it flowers
Most fair and sweetly !—O, the cloud
Of mortal sense, the living shroud
Of winged spirits, plumed by God
To traverse his celestial road !
Disfranchised, shall they find the scope
Of wisdom's undenying hope,
One day or hour the storehouse find
Of knowledge, food for deathless mind?
   Alas ! we wander with slow wings,—
The bird in sleeping sometimes sings ;
The dog barks audibly in dreams ;
Thought then is prison of its themes :

Fancy may plead with man and brute,
That each be less reserved or mute,—
The muse, though recreant to the tale,
Consents fair fancy should prevail,
Yet, hand in hand, they may attend,
Each be the faint narrator's friend.

When danger near that hamlet came,
Commissioned by the dark Segame,
Owasso sought with paces fleet
His white-browed teacher's wood-retreat:—
    'Segame—my father—Indian chief—
This morning plucked this paw-paw leaf
Which o'er his lodge the last moon grew,
A token of his heart to you!
To yonder hight from all secure,
Within a cavern's secret door,
He bids the White Dove's wings to fly,
Before this sun has left the sky ;
She there may rest when loudly sounds
The war-whoop through the hunting-grounds
Go now with me, my teacher kind,
Owasso will the panther bind,
And every beast or bird of prey
That growls or lurks along our way;
Beneath the shadows of the pines,
All silent when the day declines.
In safety your light feet shall glide,
Owasso watching by your side!

White Dove, have neither fear nor dread;
The softest furs shall be your bed,
The brightest maize, and meat, your food,
And all our wigwams yield that's good:
I'll sing when fold your wings to sleep,
And all night long safe watch I'll keep!'

Allien was calm; it was her sphere
To curb the quick tumultuous tear;
To bid unschooled emotion rest
Behind the screen.   She thus addrest
Her simple suppliant to deny
And still preserve credulity:

'I thank you, and your father-chief,—
I read his kindness in the leaf;
But come, Owasso, yet again,
When danger seems to me more plain,
And then, if needful, you shall guide
Me safely to your father's side.'

The boy was gone as light departs
When thunders flash their fiery darts.
Was anger there?   It gave no trace,
Except it be that flying pace;—
Doubt with the weight it always brings,
Questioned of trust in savage kings;
But love in that kind soul still plead,
And softened all its stings of dread,
By process old as counted time,

Invention of no age or clime,
No mathematical defense
Intangible but to one sense,
Feeling,—*of* man's fraternity—
Man's trust in man's humanity.

'Twas low and wide, that refuge cave,
Entered where on the lake's coast wave
A fissure of a frowning ledge
Yawned o'er its densely shaded edge,
Which wove a thick umbrageous door
Fringed high above with mosses hoar
That hung from granite mottled dark,
Like spotted alder's glossy bark.
  A few days more, Allien attends
Owasso, and some Christian friends,
Fleeing from savage war that nigh
Has thundered forth its bloody cry.
Noiseless along the shaded tide,
In bark canoes at eve they glide,
The Indian boy their expert guide:
No other door there seems to be
Of safety whence they now may flee,
And when each trembling refugee
Has safely passed the cavern's bound,
Something of kindness have they found;
The guests of beings strange and rude,—
Spirits of shade and solitude,—
Thinking no foe will there molest,

The hamlet band accept such rest,
Till warfare, weakened or subdued,
Pacificates a time-long feud.

    Then days move on so dim and slow
Self-burdened thought is almost woe;
Suspense its steely fetter binds
Closely around desponding minds
Whose crushed expansion feverish grows,
Consuming inward as it goes:
Imparted tidings meager seem,—
Doubt more than all disturbs the tnemo .
Of dull confinement, and the heart,
Poignant in memory, longs to part
With mortal life's inactive boon,—
The day all night, the night all noon.

God made this thousand-stringed frame
To *work*, and thus prolong the flame
Of calorific strength; refusing
Vigor and health to weak drones choosing
The latent name of life, than dowers
Exuberant with happy powers.
He bids the thinker think with hands;
The plodder use his leathern bands;
The farmer till his waiting soil;
The blacksmith strike his crimson coil
Of burning iron; the penman's arm
Prolong the hieroglyphic charm;
The weaver stock his reedy loom;

The sculptor labor for the tomb,
When Art seeks rest in beauty's bowers;
The builder hew his stated hours;—
God bids the poet seek to use
His birth-gift from the loving muse,
And know 'tis not in ideal dreams
Alone that he must choose his themes;
But he must *work* for human weal—
Must sorrow from the mourning steal,
Singing that others may inhale
Soft airs from life's Arcadian vale.
And to the painter from on high
Unfolds a book of destiny,
Which, if his soul refuse to read,
His brush will like a Nile-washed reed,
Prostrated, soiled, sunburnt and dead,
Remain when back the tide has fled.

Hence morbid sufferings come to those
Imprisoned, with their joys or woes;
Fettered but active is the mind,
Longing to *do*, each power confined
Which physical support sustains,—
Life maddening in their veins.

The hamlet's late deserted green
Bids us survey another scene;—
A captive chief condemned to die
Stands 'mid his foes, nor quails his eye
Before the fierce and proud Segame;

Bright as the sacraficial flame
Which soon around his form may rise,
It trembles not ; his soul defies
The waiting torture ; savage will,
Relentless as the rock-built hill,
Bids reason nerve the failing sense,
And pain become its own defense :
Upon his coldly rigid face   ·
His nation's stoic type we trace ;—
He asks no mercy, but desires
The speedy kindling of the fires,
While now they bind him to the tree
And round him dance in fiendish glee,
Singing a wildly warlike song,
Eager his sufferings to prolong.

Inspired by human pity sweet,
Allien comes from the cave retreat,
Her soul by heavenly impulse moved,
Serene and warm because it loved ;—
Loved not as blossoms smile in dreams ;
Loved not as sophists love their schemes ;
Loved not as envy loves to name
The pure with breathings that defame ;
Not as disputants love the feud,
Nor with vain glory's amplitude :
Her love bespoke her heart allied
To Him from out whose gentle side
Gushed forth love's pure redeeming tide.

She stands before the frowning king
A flower beneath a tree in Spring,
Pale, delicate, but trusting there,—
A spirit-bloom from Heaven's mild air !
She pleads with savage majesty,
To set the helpless victim free ;
But how she pleads we may not tell,—
Vengeance before her soft voice fell.

Woman dares all things ; few might dare
In such an hour to linger here ;
But there is strength imbedded deep
Within our souls whose forces sleep
Till danger breaks the untried wall
And spirit answers spirit's call ;
Then fear-dismantled, boldly forth
Tramples th' insignia of Earth,
And all it threatens : a new name
By that it does is but its claim :
Courage kills fear, so wave to wave
Together flowing, both are brave ;
One swells the other, they are one
When the rude rousing storm is gone.
One wing needs its attending wing ;
Spirit is dual ; if it cling
To the message breast of destiny,
Strong, and more strong, eventually
It conquers all things, flies one way,
Success and progress in its sway.

God's spirit is love, and 'tis a sword
To vanquish error's iron ccrd;
A child may use, a woman wield,
Both futile else this be their shield,
'Gainst which revenge may storm its hail;
Weakness and love may so prevail.

The Indian may relent his ire ;—
Segame forbids the kindling fire;
While yet the cloud is on his brow
He waves his hand, the chieftains bow;
Displeasure flashes, and it dies
Swift as all shades and vagaries
Disperse when mercy's lucid stream
Pours forth its countermanding beam.
   From Allien's side Owasso moves
Toward his father, whom he loves,
And by his signal cuts the bands
That hold the victim's feet and hands,
And forth he walked morosely free,
His soul saluting liberty,
As when the Deluge fiat gave
The whole world's boundary to the wave.

Time rolls along, released from war,
Refluent peace smiles near and far;
Contentment bringing brighter cheer
To every hopeful pioneer.
The Woodvale hamlet with its rude
Church structure breaks the solitude

Of isolated grove and plain ;—
Crowning its cupola, a vane,
Moving each way with silver gleam,
Signals the airs' oft changing stream.
It stands upon the central green,
And there one day a throng convene
From the surrounding region ; bands
Of missionaries join their hands,
Assembling, each from each to hear
Kind words, and gain renewing cheer.
Mingling too with the host are seen
Forms fierce in aspect, stern in mien,
Beneath whose guise the soul is wrought
To cold sublimity of thought,
Whose deep, inquiring exercise,
Buoyant with truth, may wave-like rise.
　Maidens are there whose flowing hair
Invites the fingers of the air
To toss and bend each ebon strand,
Risking no petulant command.
From brows dark as the chestnut's breast,
They vail a full, expansive chest,
Round eyes that ask the warrior's smile,
Which ne'er have drooped by flattering wile ;
O, the Indian maid is free, if cold,
Her heart unbought by pride or gold :
She roves in joy the groves among
Singing wild songs in a strange wild tongue ;
She plucks the flower, nor fears the thorn

Like tender hands to luxury born ;
Her nude brown feet plash through the wave—
When wild-beasts howl her heart is brave ;
The night, upon her couch of furs,
Brings her no ghostly visitors ;
Robust and strong, her full, glad health
Is her unguarded, wingless wealth,
And if her slumbers wake to dream,
'Tis but the lakelet's moonlight gleam.

Again we've wandered, gentle muse,
Thou canst not beauty's claims refuse !
They bring revolt, impromptu strife,
And gild the sternest phase of life ;
We hail their potency, and sigh,
And smile, and praise, with heart and eye ;—
No heart may scorn the sentient queen,—
Her power o'er man was God-forseen.

A song of praise and faith's repose
Precedes the Woodvale meeting's close ;
When, standing in the open door,
A man speaks now unheard before ;
So arbitrary his address,
It stills all impulse for egress.
A giant of his athlete race,
With flashing eyes sweeps o'er the place
One self-supporting gaze of will,
And every foot and lip are still.
Calm as an islet of the sea,

When soft airs greet it from the lea,
Like a star in twilight shining dim,
He spoke, and none upbraided him:

'Brothers ! The Red-man's home is happy—herds
Of buffalo roam through his hunting-grounds—
They wait his arrow in the river-vale ;
The deer starts up before him in the shades,
The beaver and the otter give their furs   '
To warm him in the Winter's cold. To cheer
His heart the prairies bloom—the showers come
Upon the waiting earth—the maize springs up
To bear its yellow grains and give him food.—
The winds of night perfume the red-man's lodge—
Long, long the moons have blest his forest home !
When his Great Father bids him cross the stream
Beyond the sunset dim—far, far away,
To those green hunting-grounds where trees ne'er drop
Their leaves, his bones in our fair valleys rest—
Birds sing around his grave !—Ontara must
Be heard—he says a mighty voice calls back
The warriors to worship Manito !
The pale-face has a God—his God is not
The Indian's Father. Hear ! Return—come back,
Brave brothers, to the love of Manito !'

He ceased ; and ere each swarthy breast
Through faith or apathy's attest
Grows fervent in belief, or chill
As the inactive frost-bound rill ;

Or minds less dark protest the claim
Of superstition's waning flame,
Chanting a low, triumphant song,
Ontara slowly leaves the throng.
And we from this closed scene away
Through unfrequented paths will stray;
We thread the grove, the village bound,
Walk musing by a burial-ground,
Where spreads a field of ripening grain,
And farther, reach a shadeless plain;
From thence our steps salute a dell—
So dense its shade, there broods a spell
Prophetic of some future night,
Quelling,—compelling the quick flight
Of fancy's sunny wing, to bind
A dark-hued chaplet round the mind.

Come, ye who love the solemn wood,
And the mute airs of solitude,
Where God the all-pervading reigns,
Where thought accepts the unseen chains
Binding it to the Infinite,
Prescient of uninvaded light!
Worn pathway this, and scarcely seen,
So lace the boughs their twigs between;
Slowly and more slow we tread
O'er vanquished trunks, moss-grown as dead;
Bend back the shades—no sunbeam dwells
In these old barricaded cells,
Vast labyrinths where dryads dance,

And elfins court their changing glance;
The spell grows deeper, like the hush
Of earthquake pause, or thought's quelled rush
Preceding passion's tumult dark,
When angels of the conscience hark
To nature's warning, bidding fear
Be retribution's harbinger.

Deep, deep descending, dim and drear,
Ontara's home our steps are near :
When noon is at its hight, one smile
Of sunny day these shades beguile,—
The beam falls now on the 'Prophet's' hair—
Behold him stand majestic there,
Like one bereft, whose memory dwells
In complaining shrines like sighing shells!
He seems to mourn, yet not to mourn,
As though his soul some weight had borne—
Some natural grief, concealed too well,
Which nothing outward may dispel.
But what sometimes most real seems
Is but like dreams recalling dreams
Gone when the charmed mind essays
To fasten their etherial rays!
So if we ask, we may in vain
The source of his peculiar pain ;—
The seer grieves not for visions past,
Prophetic gleams that would not last,
So dark the cloud, so weak the light
Struggling to break his mental night,

That not one foreign grasp may try
To fix its tangibility ;
Far denser now than shades that closed
Around the babe when it reposed
Upon its tawny mother's breast,
Where smiles bent rarely on its rest,
When superstition's power began
To appropriate the growing man,
And ignorance ne'er left his side
While months to years were multiplied.

Is there no force to break the bands,
And give the soul its full demands,
E'en though like Saul, when prostrate falling,
Sudden and strange its spirit-calling ?
May not the rudest type of man
Wisdom and truth be taught to scan ?
Thank Heaven, and Love, and Light, for this,
The heathen may receive the bliss
Of intellectual progress !   All
On whom God's effluence may fall,
Howe'er debased, may leave behind
The deadly wilderness of mind.

An image moves the Prophet's brain ;
'I must see the pale-face maid again !
Whence came this bird of tender wing ?
Her voice is like the sigh of Spring—
She breathes upon the Indian child—
His heart before untaught and wild,

Unused to smiles and tender love,
Becomes the playmate for the dove!
Great Manito! whence comes the power
Of one so frail—the white young flower?'
    Swelling like seas or unquelled fires,
Like growing winds or fed desires,—
Conflict ideal, impetuous strife
Becomes the spur of his wild life;
But yet he fails to comprehend
How waves may with the ether blend—
The mortal with the spirit:—There's
O'er the living tide that bears
His thought unguided to the sea
Of wisdom's far immensity,
Mysterious breezes whispering tales
Of unknown shores and untried sails,
Which his lone bark may gain at last,
And with their anchors his be cast.
    He sees us not. O, break not now
This spell by sound or whisper low!
Truth conquers in God's season. Fret
Not thou the arrow rankling yet
In an immortal's bosom, when
His depth of pain is 'neath thy ken,
But wait the Spirit's indication
When thou may'st speak of Christ's salvation.

There's none to meet the seer when come
At night or morn to his bark home;

7   J

He lives alone ; no wife or child
Irradiates his prison-wild ;
Nor may we nearer pass to view
The spot where never Saxon shoe
Has wended :—Cautious, we retrace
The dark, almost impervious lace
Of silent nature's cunning fingers,
But as we go the Spirit lingers ;
Too damp, umbrageous and too weird
This place for souls with earth attired.

A day is gone,—another scene
Less wild, less calm, no less serene,
Imprinted on the virgin page,
Fair fancy's favor may engage.
   Bright sunbeams through an open door
Fall on a rough but leaf-strewn floor,
And there's a group with eyes intent,—
Some wandering glances idly spent,—
Some ears tuned save to nature's tones,—
The water's dash, the forest-moans,
The hawk's blank note, the blue-jay's scream,
Or thunders rending childhood's dream ;—
Within the circle one more fair,
With gentle eye and sunny hair,
With rose and lily on her cheeks,
In soft convincing fervor speaks :
She talks scarce in her native tongue ;
Most like an incoherent song

Of early childhood are the swells
Of English monosyllables,
Commingling with the medium grand—
The natural voice of that young band.
 Another comes ! 'Tis none but he,
The prophet of the deepening eye :
His dress is not the warrior's guise;
Unplumed his brow ; a strange device
Of quills and shells adorns his breast,
Which vibrates slowly in its rest.

'Maiden ! Ontara speaks ! He comes in peace !
The White Dove's wing stirs all the forest leaves—
She finds the prophet's home—her smile is like
The setting sun—it leaves upon his heart
A shadow dark—it tells of night—the night
Of Manito ! The morning—shall it break?—
Her words are voices of the singing wood—
They come—but whence ! Ontara may not see !
They whisper of the " Savior-God" and sing
Of "Heaven"—her story to the hunter tribes—
Great Manito has sent it not ! He will
Restrain his curse—he will not harm the Dove !
But, maiden, hear ! There comes a cloud afar—
Ontara hears its thunders roar—'t will break
Upon the pale-face—let him now forsake
The red-man's home, and leave him to his God !
The Dove flies back to her safe nest to warn
Her people of the curse of Manito !'

With softly firm, convincing tone,
She answers thus the earnest one :—
'Ontara has a heart sincere,—
To him these little ones are dear;
From far away for love I came
To tell them Jesus' holy name;
He is the son of Manito,
Who came to live with men below,
Leaving his Heavenly Father's throne
To live in sorrow and alone;
And die in pain that man might be
Happy in all eternity !
Ontara will believe in Him,
And then his soul that now is dim
Shall be all love, and peace, and light,
And sin no more shall cloud his sight.'

Superstition, truth by chance
Enrobed in doubt and ignorance ;
The dark mind's dream of destiny ;—
Its horror of obscurity :
Despise it not, nor deprecate
Its origin and ultimate ;
Transport it from its earthly load
On wings of light, to Christ and God.

The seer ignores the teacher's tone,-
One silent moment, he has gone ;
With rapid pace, almost with wings,
He speeds and up a bold cliff springs ;

Confused the tumult of his mind,—
He rushes on, he talks, the wind
Invokes, the trees, the sky; his frown
Dispels the rays that gliding down
Impenetrate the umbrage wild,
And aggravate this recluse child:
Now as with him to sympathize,
Clouds are concentring in the skies,
Darkening around the distant hills
Whose hearts sustain migrating rills;
Storm-forces marshal mute and fast,
The tree-bound arch is overcast;—
Ontara 'merges from the wood,
Alone, unlinked in brotherhood
With social being; all around
Is solitary—God 's profound!
The vocal bird has lost his note;
Silent the whispering insect's throat;
Each shrub and tree in shadow vailed,
The trembling wild-flower's cheek is paled:—
Troubling the ripples of the lake,
Nearer the transient thunders break,
And from their viewless fragments dark
Fly flames and brief electric spark;
Wind-currents sweep from vale to vale;
Accelerating, the wild gale
Compels allegiance everywhere,
From wood and water, earth and air .
Boughs forced to move, their rigid nerves

Describe new angles, figures, curves;
While many a tissued bower is rent,
And broken branches flying sent.
And now the storm's prolonging roar
Commands rain-torrents down to pour,
And the o'erwhelming conflict seems
Designed to waste th' aerial streams.

Amid this elemental strife
Of force unseen, and opaque life,
As if bereft of all design,
Standing beneath a slender pine,
Unbowed in attitude, the seer
In scorn of tenderness or fear,
Ever a stranger to alarm,
Awaits the issue of the storm;
His arms are thrown across his breast
As if to bind his life's unrest;
So deep his thought, so deep his eyes
Conceal the fire that in them lies,
The soul enthrallment yet unbroken
Discovers no explaining token.
He starts as if at once to fly
A spirit's contiguity!
But soon expression lifts the band,
Voice-tones o'er thought's domain command;
And while spent nature slacks its chain,
Abating wind and hail and rain,
With dignate, measured step he walks,

And to his own attendance talks ;
His words his own complacent ear
Deems eloquent as they're sincere ;
As calm as earnest, now they claim
Truth's semblance, truth to him, the same
As more enlightened minds may grasp,—
Light foiling error's subtle clasp !
    He talks of a grim cavern, where
He knows the spirit will declare
As oft to his lone ear before
The Mighty Father's awful power ?
A wondrous cave, where silence dwells,
Where darkness knows no light farewells ;
Where bird, nor beast, nor living thing
Has breath, or pulse, or sense, or wing !—
Realm of uncultured magnitude—
Pathway to Earth's heart solitude !
    'Ill lead the tender maiden there—
She must the Spirit's answers hear :
The whisper and the thunder tone
Proclaiming Manito is ONE !
She then will heed Ontara's word,
And talk no more of Saviour-Lord !
Her legend, like the morning rain,
Will pass, nor blind her eyes again !'

Shadows are stealing, longer lines
Creep toward the East :—the day declines ;
The prairie's rainbow hues grow dim ;
The horizon binds a purple rim

Around a sleep-preparing world ;
The hamlet's smoke is skyward curled ;
. The whip-poor-will attunes his note,
Aromas from the flower-cups float.

Allien has wandered forth to share
The soft enchantments of the air ;—
A scene too fair and pure to last,
Her vision welcomes from the past
Whose mystic process—nature wrought—
Is now the alchemy of thought.

Her path winds toward a forest rill
Where fays their nectar cups might fill,
Those fabled sprites credented long
To live on air and breathe in song !

Dim shades are gathering ; far and wide
More cool contracts the aerial tide,—
Low lullabys entrance the sense
Through mother Nature's happiness.
Our fairy sits beside the stream
Where eddying circles drown the gleam,
And crimp the shadowed outlines spread
From sycamores far o'er her head.
Responsive to rapt evening's powers,
She loses sense of passing hours ;
Nor till the birds' last notes are hushed,
And by her side the grass is brushed
By human feet, does she arouse,
Not fearful, but to learn the cause
Of interruption, stir, or sound,

When life to her is so profound.
Is it the genius of the glade?—
Ontara stands before the maid.
Rebuking now her pensive mood,
She breaks the silence of the wood
By tones whose soft and cheery swell
No tremblings of surprises tell:
Smiling she points to the evening star,
Sparkling 'tween foliage curve and bar,
And asks the prophet what they are—
Those lights above the Indian's home,
Guiding his feet when far they roam.

He gazes skyward, then his eyes,
As when the lightning's arrow flies,
Are drooping—darkened: he is blind.
O, there's a wilderness of mind
More dark than Huron's fir-black groves,
Where stealthily the panther roves ;
To liberate its captive shore,
'Where serpents hiss and monsters roar,'
Where th' Infinite delays to dawn
O'er thought's chaos, creation's morn ;.
To wrest it from piratic bands
Of sin and ignorance, whose hands
Would chain it from progression's strife,
Were glory for the longest life !
Allien is pondering, waiting still
The answer of Ontara's will ;
7*

But stands in silence that dark one,—
To *anarchy* his thoughts have run !

*　　*　　*　　*　　*

Alas ! diverted from our theme,—
Patience, kind reader, 'tis no dream !
A word has burst the pent-up tide
Of patriotic love and pride ;
Has sorrow's urn unwreathed to view,
Where fall yet undisturbed, anew,
The distillations of a heart
That cannot bid the cause depart :—
Pardon we need not ask of thee,
The awful, dread reality,
Long ere this simple page may meet
Thy frowning glance or favor sweet,
May change a nation's destiny,
And choke with blood its onward way !
May wring a million hearts with woe,
And through its own inherent foe !

Alas ! my native land, that thou
To direful civil war must bow !
That brother must 'gainst brother stand,
To sever such a starry band !
That o'er our fair dishonored STATES
The Angel of Doom now darkly waits !*
That wild Rebellion reckless pours

* March, 1861.

Disgraceful ruin on our shores !
Is there no intervening power
To give Hope's prescience to the hour—
To dissipate portending death,
And quell Columbia's fever-breath?

Unfold we not the sealed scroll
O'er whose spread page the years may toll
Undying requiems for the slain
Of many a red rebuking plain ;
But hear you not faint moans from far,
Nature's combined regrets for war,—
The knell of hearts too true and brave
To stand inert around the grave
Of freedom's proud fraternity,
And see her banded Empire lie
Vanquished, for History's long scorn,
Bidding no more Republics born?
We wait the issue : Heaven ! how long?—
O burden of the patriot's song !—

*   *   *   *   *   *

Return we to our former strain,
Salute remoter scenes again :
The seer, as if his soul were blind,
As if he felt the blight of mind,
No answer gave :—Allien now bends
To seek the path that homeward tends,
While no weak fears her heart betide ;—

Ontara moving by her side,
She asks the Indian name for trees,
For sky, for cloud, for evening breeze,
And thus diverts the conflict crude
Which agitates his nature rude,
Calming the life-tides of his breast
Though dark as ocean be their rest,
Surging far down through unknown deep,
'Neath surface calms that briefly sleep.

At length they reach the cheerful cot,
Her mission home, a friendly spot;
Beneath the stars' fraternal light
She turns to bid the sage 'good-night;'
Moving her hand with gentle art,
A signal that he now depart:
But his demeanor, urgent, strong,
The interview would yet prolong;
And while her eyes bend on him still,
As if to fathom that dark will,
As if she were less fair and frail,
He speaks; and 'tis no gentle tale
Of love or friendship, rest or hope,
With which her doubting heart might cope;
He tells her of that distant cave
Where breaks no sound of life — the grave
Of noiseless airs and waters dim,
Where the Spirit oft has answered him!
Ontara there will test the plan
And story of the Savior-man;

Will to her willing senses show,
By words sent forth from Manito,
That all is false, and but a dream
Like glow-worms o'er a darkened stream.
If she with him will seek the cave,
The prophet's trust she thus will save !
His broken words his meaning tells
Imparted from a breast that swells
With more than innate savage pride ;
For that pure being by his side
Is kindred by Creative Hand,
And weaves around his grosser mind
Soft powers to it all undefined.
So pearl-like pebbles, and opaque,
And sandy ones the waves may break
Mingle upon the ocean's shore,
In brotherhood forevermore.

What means the Indian's strange request?
His purpose has sincere attest !
There's for his faith some natural cause,
Fulfillment of Jehovah's laws ;—
There may be sound of falling wave
Remote, unseen, within the cave,
Or some weird echo may perchance
The listening prophet's soul entrance ;
And these may Heaven's forerunners bo
Of truth in mystic imagery,
When scales shall fall from unbound eyes

Before redemption's mysteries.
    Allien fears nothing by his side,—
Would safely trust him as her guide;
Nor is her faith in him so rare,
For woman's trust is everywhere.

The seer departed undenied,
The morn's conclusion to abide:
Allien is musing while a cloud
Draws o'er the rising moon its shroud,
Mute memory hails the long ago—
'*Go forth, my child, to duty go!*'
An angel mother's soul again
Had breathed its soft persuasive strain,
Approaching from her Heavenly sphere,
Her child's still tender minister;
And she assenting falters not,
Resolves to seek the mystic grot,
Ere morn for noonday's glare recedes,
To follow where Ontara leads.

'Tis Autumn :—'Twas but yesternight
The Summer sun withdrew its light,
Yet bright with morn Apollo rose,
In harvest promise, to disclose
Light's corresponding rainbow crest
Wreathing the circle of the west.
While dews and sweets of flowers are blending
The maiden and her guide are wending,
Earnest, alone, their forest way,—

They roam as nature's children stray,
Where streamlets babble cheerily,
Where fawn and squirrel bounding free,
Disturb not the song-birds' melody.

Four days they journey through the wild ;—
Each night Ontara fagots   piled,   .
Whose friendly flames dispersed the gloom,
And checked the owl's dolorous tune.
    At midnight, when the panther's scream
Broke on her half-remembered dream,
Or the wild-cat rent the stilly air
Like some lone goblin of despair,
Allien, upon her couch of boughs,
Affrighted briefly, feared the cause ;
Perception quickened, fine, intense,
Attenuating every sense,
Until the potency of prayer
Brought peace, and home, and safety there.

Morning !   Glad harbinger of truth !
Beauty and health, perpetual youth,
Inspire thy soul, illume thy brow,
Which bids the sorrowing disavow
Misanthropy and discontent,—
Grief's absolute abandonment.
No hand so bountiful as thine,
Can Peace invoke to deck her shrine
With lillies fair and spirituelle,

Olive, and bay, and immortelle!
Advancing on their cheerful way,
They reach a bluff ere noon of day,
Where by Missouri's restless side
A birch canoe is safely tied:
Coast gliding slowly with one oar,
One mild, forgetful hour or more,
They landed where the waters lave
The time-wrought bulwarks of the cave;
Near where the 'Father's' noble breast
Accepts the rival, wave-carest;
Where Mississippi's northern blue
Receives another's staining hue;
But still for many a mile sustains
Preponderating azure veins;
E'en as pure souls resisting long,
Weary before temptation strong,
When nevermore their vestal birth
Repudiates the stain of Earth.
Here far as vision may descry
Behold a wild sublimity!
Huge trees, gray, angulated rocks,
Fragments of post-diluvian shocks,
Gnarled trunks uptorn by Borean powers,
Green matted brush and straggling flowers,
O'erhanging vines and lichens red,
And mosses like crimped emeralds spread,—
In thick profusion thrown and grown,
To art's chaste empire all unknown.

The bird of many voices* sung;
The jay's shrill note through shadows rung;
The oriole's charming lay,
Uniting with the red-bird gay,
Composed an Orphean roundelay.

Now clambering down a shelving rocky plane,
They pass within a dim and strange domain
Meeting contesting airs and currents chill,
Which to the frame impart a feverish thrill;—
No silver-clouded or cerulean skies
Shed lusters on their path; ungemmed it lies
Where never springs the dew-invoking grass
The rainbow's emerald glories to surpass:
No stir of breeze, no hum of insect throng,—
Sound! sound! There is no sound. 'Tis death—
The stillness that succeeds departed breath.
Is danger here? No specter haunts the eye;
Shades of no living monsters they descry,
But all along their rocky, winding way,
Bold fragments, relics grand their eyes survey:
Vast broken column, dark worn battlement,
Which struggled while the shaft of ages spent
Its purpose, with the constant flowing wave,
Extending slow the region of the cave.
Rude corridors and arches huge behold,
Where royal diamonds never flashed in gold;

*The American bird of many voices, that laughs at the eloquence of
man.—Wilson's 'Tales of the Border and of Scotland.'

Where pleasure's purple wine-cups never foamed;
Where beauty's dancing foot-fall never roamed!
Beneath yon nature-frescoed roof no sound
Of revel ever broke the cool profound,
Since conquering darkness spread its empire far,
Unsoftened by one ray of moon or star.   .
And till the subtle force Jehovah wields
Plows up again these subterranean fields,
The casual torch and feeble, lights alone
This wondrous handiwork of days unknown!—
If known to history 'tis now forgot;
The fire of prophecy illumed it not,—
A page chronology may never claim,
But on that lofty frieze behold its Maker's name!

In period remote these chambers grim,
Defiant, shouted their chaotic hymn,   .
When sleeping forces moved their unpent bound,
And wandering left no record to expound.
These rocks are symbols of His power—
The Wonderful, who reared the mountain's tower;-
God's autographs on nature's unsealed scroll
Which ne'er to human vision may unroll.
O, endless mysteries!   O, dreadful gloom!
O, tenfold dread of death and such a tomb!
Hence, spectral thoughts! Ye fancies crude, retire,-
Enkindle not the mind's consuming fire!

Ontara and Allien descend, or climb,
In silence and oblivious of time,

Until their torches cast their lurid quiver
Across a dark, a still, Lethean river,
Which frowns upon their way as though its glide
Came from the depths of Hades terrified !—
Embarking in a low canoe, they pass
Slowly across its plane of ebon glass,
Between vast mural walls, stern, jagged, gray,
A hundred fathoms 'neath the realm of day !

Allien is solemn ; slow the paddle's dip
Impels the mimic solitary ship,
While superstition's all-controlling trance
Enchains the dark Ontara's lip and glance.
She sings, 'Praise God from whom all blessings flow
———— Praise him all creatures here *below.*'
The human harmony an instant gone,
Returns with loud-toned echoes, on and on
Each note and word repeated o'er and o'er,
Makes populous the arch, and wave, and shore.

And now they reach a pebbly strand,
Whereon their careful footsteps land ;—
Tracing a wilder rocky way,
A narrower path, still on they stray ;
No question from Allien disclosing
Late thoughts of danger ; still reposing
On Heaven's protecting arm, she bears
Within her soul her few faint fears.
Murmuring some broken accents low,
Somber the leader pauses now,

Where huge stalactites, roughly grooved,
Have age on age remained unmoved,
Old mile-stones for the monster gnomes
Who hasted to their unknown homes,
When lame disorder, wild and glad,
Raved unrebuked, demoniac, mad,
Perchance before Creation's morn,
Ere Earth's young loveliness was born.

The prophet stands by one rough base,
Determined purpose in his face ;
Concealing well his soul's unrest,
Invokes the spirit-proven test :
His left arm lain upon the shaft,
His right upraised as if to waft
The invocation up to Heaven,—
His voice the dark still air has riven :—

'Art thou alone, great Manito ?'
The echo answers, ' *Manito.*'
With firmer tone he speaks again,
And louder swells th' inquiring strain :
'Great Manito, he is but one !'
' *Great Manito, he is but one.*'
And now a whisper moves his tongue ;
Those far retreating aisles among
The gentle answer come in strains,
Of wild, mysterious refrains :
'The Christian legend—it is false !'
' *The Christian legend—it is false.*'

Now by the torches' unfixed gleaming,
Allien discerns th' exultant beaming
Of soul-wrought eyes, dark orbs of pride,
Which confutation's power defied ;—
And then his voice the silence breaks :
'The White Dove hears — the Mighty speaks !'

A moment mute, her soul in prayer,
His young companion asks still there
The omnipresent God to send
His spirit error's bonds to rend ;
Then with no weak or trembling tones,
But more of strength than woman owns
When cherished by affection's care,
Breathing 'sweet home's' protecting air,
She lays her hand upon the stone,
Repeating, 'Jesus is the Son,'—
The echo answers, '*is the Son*,'—   .
'Of God, the Christian's Manito,
Who came to save the world from woe.'
' *Who came to save the world from woe.*'
She whispers, 'Is the story true?'
A murmur says, '*the story true.*'

 ✳ ✳ ✳ ✳ ✳ ✳

Still as may sleep a buried wave,
Silent and somber as the cave,
With no reflex of heavens blue,
Ontara from the darkness drew,

With leading step the tired Allien,
Who longed for visions bright and green ;
As from the cavern they emerge,
Low sunbeams from the western verge
Illume the vistas of the wood,
Enlivening all the solitude :
Wild nature's charms have treble power
In that appreciative hour ;
Beauty withdrawn, three-fold the more
'Tis loved in memory than before.
Bewildered by the darkness' loss
She sinks upon a bed of moss,
Still watching his averted look
Or transient glance, as though a book
Revealed to her inquiring eye
Erudite truth or mystery.

   Stern, fixed, unyielding, proud,
The seer there stands with head unbowed ;—
Forbidding overture, or tone
Remonstrative, by his dark frown :—
A sudden change,—O, strange compelling !
A softer influence upward welling ;
Another formula now tells
His thought's new oracles !

'The eagle's ear may list a voice that flows
  Like Minnehaha's silver singing tide ;
As mild as Cautantow ;'

* The south-west wind.

The Indian-Summer when the streams are wide!'

Bowing to his sincerity,
O'erwearied, she defers reply,
But bids him kindly then prepare
The meal of which she needs to share;
And soon the simple task is done,—
Shaved morsels of dried venison,
Honey and cakes of pounded corn,
Answers the want with nature born:
And soon the tent of fur is spread,
'Neath which a fair and trusting head
Laid on a pillow of pine leaves,
Her safety to Jehovah gives.
Dry boughs are kindled, then the seer
Lies down to healthful slumber near,
A tree his canopy, the ground
The softest couch he would have found.

The dawn has wasted, wanes the day;
They 've wandered far upon their way:—
Ontara moody strides along,
The maiden's voice breaks forth in song;
A song of home, of the bright, brief past,
Ere her early sky was overcast:
The opening notes were warbled slow,
Her peaceful soul's most natural flow;
But soon, as if some stronger thought
Her sensibilities inwrought,
More loud and free rang out the sound

In the choral's rich, melodious bound :
The cadence floating distant clear,
Fell softly on a fainting ear ;
'I hear an angel's rapturous tone,'
Murmured a lone and dying one.

Ceases the song ; still on they bear ;
The travelers fear no danger there ;
They pause before a fern-loved rill,—
Is it their drinking-cups to fill?
What chains the prophet's sable eyes ?
The mute Allien—what her surprise?
Is the panther near, crouched low to slay
His unoffending human prey ?
Or human foe has Ontara seen,
In ambush through th' imperfect screen?
    Their pause is brief: they 're moving now,—
Observe the gentler being bow
Beside a fair and wasted form,
Whose nerveless hands with faint life warm,
Upon her panting bosom prest,
Give soothing sense to its unrest.

'Speak, sister—'tis a friend would know
Thy name, thy home, perchance thy woe !
O tell me, has a treacherous hand
Conveyed thee from thy native land?
Look up, dear girl: discard thy fear—
Speak low, and I each word will hear ;
Whisper thy tale of joy or pain,

And God may give thee strength again !'

A look that Heaven and Earth combined
Revealed the power of each enshrined
In that sad soul, serene and young ;
A few faint words escaped her tongue,
Meeting like unseen waves of air
A corresponsive answering there ;
Enlivening by the love she felt
Warming in her who o'er her knelt.

My home is near across the glade
Musing but weak, too far I strayed ;
The only home I have below'—
I talk not of another now :
'Tis an Indian's roof that shelters me,
But far away I soon shall be ;—
Hast thou come from that celestial land,
Leaving, for love, thy angel band ?'

Silent, Ontara waiting by,
Watches the twain with wondering eye,
Disturbing not the holy scene,
Till by a signal from Allien]
He moves to bend his athlete form,
And bind each dusky sinewy arm
Around the fragile, stricken girl,
While toys the air with each soft curl
That backward falls from her classic head,—
To bear her on with careful tread :

8

Her attendant walks so gently by,
The sufferer's heart forgets to sigh;
Soon through the lowly cottage door
They pass, the one to pass no more,
Save what remains when life has fled.
　Gathered around that dying bed,
Expressionless some dark ones stood;
Statues, not souls of brotherhood,
So mute, so cold, so fixed in mien,—
So tearless by that tearful scene!
Passion concealed, it bore no trace
In lineaments of the warrior face;
And, dark-browed too the matron sat,
Watching the maiden's dying fate.
The pale one moves as if to speak,
Her closing eyes, but O, so weak!
Another bends her ear more low,
Catching the fading tones that flow
In whispers from those lips as white
As roses in the moon's pale light,
And broken like a dream of song,—
A half-told tale of sorrowing long:

'Maiden, I know not who thou art,
But, oh! thou hast a kindly heart!
Like sister Bertha, lost, and dear,'—
Her eyes are dimmed with love's last tear,—
'Like her thy voice and manner are;—
O, I have seen thee oft afar!

She died beneath the skies of France
When vines were green in Summer's glance:
Exiles from our delightful land,
My parents joined a pilgrim band;—
They 'scaped the ocean's furious wave,
The river its cold burial gave,
Far toward the South, where, broad and deep,
Its curving currents proudly sweep,
Wandering in grace and power around
A hamlet and a lofty mound.
I, clinging to a floating oar,
Was wafted to the stranger shore,—

*   *   *   *   *   *

Kindly this cot has sheltered me,
But years have worn, oh ! gloomily,—
Now all is well ; rejoice the same,
Though marble never know my name;
'Tis thine to keep, to speak no more,—
At home they called me Isidore ;—
Now memories flash their bright brief spell
From my beautiful past I loved too well !—
Adieu, adieu,— O, thou hast come
To plant wild flowerets on my tomb,
And we shall meet above the skies,
Robed in the bloom of Paradise !'

The faint voice ceased, another tone
Breathed softly near the dying one;

An angel melody of prayer,
Bringing the court of Heaven there:
Clasping the lingerer's thin hand,
As though of one ethereal band,
Together they might hail the spheres
That roll beyond the Vale of Tears,
Allien invoked eternal peace,
And for that soul a calm release.

The prophet stood in awe that proved
His being by that death-scene moved;
Softened by supplication's breath,
Which told of Christian hope in death,'
Till borne on faith's upbearing tide,
Prayer's last aspiring murmur died
To mortal's gross discernment, while
Angelic legions caught its smile:
Life's faintest quiver alternates
With death's, till each abates
Their visual uncertainties
And the untrammeled spirit flies
Where no return a tale hath spoken,—
Earth's native links forever broken.

Gently the forest turf is laid
· On the mortal rest of the lovely maid,
While wildly floats an Indian song
From the solemn lips of that dark throng;
The homeless one is left to sleep
Where flickering rays through wood shades creep,

From year to year, from Spring to Spring ;
Where no loved one's hand shall ever bring
A wreath of flowers, or urn of tears,
Till the resurrection morn appears.

Two days have told their beading hours,
No cloud o'er the sea of sunset lowers ;
Wrapped in the twilight's soft gray gloam,
Our travelers have found their home.
Morn wakes again, great freedom's voice
Bids all the powers of life rejoice ;—
The Autumn's shortening pathway tells
Retiring beauty's new farewells.
    Owasso wanders forth to greet
His teacher with an offering sweet,
Of blossom wild and fragrant bough,
His heart entranced he knows not how :
They meet, now where the brooklet turns
To hide its silver 'neath the ferns,
Pleased recognition in each eye ;—
Something of love and gallantry
Inspires bestowal of the gift,
Gathered from wood and rocky rift.
    Ontara too—he comes again,
And spirit-broken seems his strain :
His forest home is meager now
To satisfy thought's higher flow,
Whose new demand is like a tide
That bursts a mountain basin's side,

And disintegrates sand or rock,
To scatter for its vapory flock,
Rushing to valley freedom, where,
Sun-kissed, it gilds the ambient air.

'White Dove! Ontara speaks again—his heart
Is moved—there's darkness yet, but morning comes!
The Indian's Manito no more looks down.
The voices of the pines are not his tones!
The sunshine darkens—where is Manito?
The talking of the waters—his no more
The prophet's pathway through the lonely wood—
'Tis like the trail of death.   Maiden! 'T will end.
The Son of God—he answered in the cave!
Ontara's pride is broken—he believes!
The Christian maiden died in peace—in light!
A brighter land is her's;—Dark, dark—
Ontara's way is cloud—he sees the light
Afar!   The Christian's God is his—he prays!'

The boy has listened; simplest speech
That may their comprehension reach
Is from the teacher meek and mild,
Addressed the man, heard by the child.
   She talks of Jesus:—How can one
So young, so tender, so alone,
So frail and mortal, take the theme
Of love-redeeming, and of Him,
Man's everlasting friend, discourse
With such enlightening, kindling force?

How ask me! His pure lips have said,
When he for our salvation bled,
'As the great Father loves the Son,
So ye who love, in me are one!'
And, 'Whatsoe'er ye ask in me
In faith believing, ye shall see!"
   For Him who blushed the wave to wine;
Who made blind eyes awake and shine;
Who called dead Lazarus from his grave,
And childhood's flesh of beauty gave
To leprosy; who, on the cross
Of agony, forgave man's loss
Of pity, kindness, faith and love,
And bade the thief find joy above;
Whose acts were miracles, whose word
Is wisdom,—for this sovereign Lord,
By truth's perpetual certain rays,
To fill that Indian's soul with grace,
Think you it were a marvel task?
'Tis almost sin that thus we ask.

With life, and bloom, and music-tone,
Joy-ladened Spring comes speeding on;—
Month after month has worn away.
Since sunset claimed that Autumn day
When first the Indian prophet's voice
Proclaimed the Savior-Lord his choice,
And true, his soul from that glad hour,
Has proved the Spirit's wakening power.

Woodvale awoke one fragrant morn,
Some with the sun, some with the dawn,
Both young and old, morose or gay,
To welcome those from far away:
Before the rustic church has been
A platform spread upon the green,
And simple rough-hewn seats await
The band that thither congregate.

Fragrant and soft the vernal air
Kisses the heads uncovered there,
Resting on braid or curling-hair.
Age o'er some brows a silvery wreath
Of luster adds to lids beneath,
And bronzed and sunken cheeks present
Luxury's long abandonment.
　　Missionaries gathered to confer,
And each the other's work to cheer;
Hunters—a few from wilds remote
Have come on foot, or rowed in boat—
From log-built homes the pioneer;
Indians from haunts afar, or near;
Matrons, and maids, and children young,
Diverse in beauty, week and strong;—
Allien is there,—a few dim years
Have left no trace of sorrow's tears;
Her life's content has given employ
To perfect peace, preserving joy,
Which gem-like from youth's casket throws

A prism wreath of dazzling glows.

In readiness, th' assembled throng
Unite their varied powers for song,
A simple lay that breathes of love
Redeeming, and its home above:
It closes; brief the concert-pause,
When words unasked abruptly rose :—

'Ontara, prophet of the tribes, has come —
He tells Jehovah's children of his peace!
The white-man's God in his.   Allien — the dove
Of Manito — the Christian maid — she spoke.
Jesus, the Son of Manito, looks down ;—
He gives the voice of prayer.   Her love — it broke
The darkness of Ontara's soul.   'Tis light ! —
Red brothers, hear the words of truth !   Believe !
This light will save my people — they must pray.
God, the Great Spirit, will forgive their sins —
His Son will save their souls from death !'

He ceased: Still do his eyes the scene survey
And rest on her who taught his lips to pray ;
Then strangely to her ear a soft, sweet tone
Came back as half-forgotten songs return :—
'*Allien! The diamond in the darkest mine
Forgets not ever it has power to shine!*'
The words, though like a sudden sorcery
Breaking the passing hour's serenity,
Produced no fainting, no impulsive rush

8*   L

Of recognition, but a silent flush
Of unexpected pleasure, while the past
In panoramic motion overcast
The much-changed present, all its joy, its grief,
Its hopes, that faded like an August leaf,
Illumined through her heart's o'ermantling screen,
Succeeded each the other, and *the might have been!*
Yes, Mortimer was there!   His pensive brow
Still fair as when he breathed his early vow ;
His deep blue eyes, as eloquent, still told
His unstained manhood,—all they could unfold.

The moon had risen.   Peace abroad
Walked viewless o'er the mead and road,
Mingling its glow with Luna's sheen,
Like love and joy, for sweet Allien,
Companions traced the same smooth way,
As they had walked one by-gone day,
Though rarer now to each they speak
In whispers near each other's cheek,
Till rest they on a moss-grown rock,
O'er which a widely branching oak
Sustains its shadow ;—'tis not night
To hearts so filled with love's delight !

'Allien, that morning long ago,
Whose memory, like the sun-kissed flow
Of valley streams, to me has been,
Through pain and cloud, a hallowed scene ;—
Comes it not back this night to thee,

With love's asserting potency?
O, tell me, sweet, didst thou forget
The wanderer who loves thee yet?—
O, since my heart's warm tendrils clung
Round thee, my gentler self, I've sung
One strain in all my thoughts of love :—
'Allien is mine, we'll meet above !'
Now God has blessed my thorny way
And crowned it with this joyous day.

 Yes, dearest, He who strung love's lyre,
Who kindled its immortal fire,
Uniting hearts by living ties
To live as one in Paradise,
Mid error, disappointment, death,
Pure love—the essence of His breath—
Has indestructible, eternal made ;
'Tis not a casual theme unweighed
By soul-intelligence and power ;
It dies not like a withering flower,—
It is the music of the spheres,
And knows not country, home, nor years
If these essay to break, or part
Fond souls that beat as one warm heart ;
Commingling like two clouds of even,
When two in one begin their Heaven!

 Dear angel of my waiting years !
Pearls rare and priceless are these tears ;
Giving my heart a full consent
To bliss united—love's content.

Strange prescience of this hour was mine
When, unrebuked, my heart would twine
Wreaths, flowery structures, shadowy bloom,
Dispelling all the present's gloom !
Now, blest reality, I claim
No richer gift, no boon of fame ;
Kind Heaven has sent thee to my arms,
And life and earth renew their charms !'

She answers him :—'I did not know
I loved you in that long ago ;
My morning years were chilled with gloom,
When called to mourn each parent's tomb,
And youth's first blight of early love ;
But I have looked for rest above.
When first I met thy gentle smile
On life's dim sea, it was an isle
Of beauty,— an oasis green
Upon the desert's burning sheen :
Not then I knew its untried power ,
Not then I thought of this sweet hour :
My inexpressive being dwelt
In dreamy vistas ; it had felt
A natural love's youth-pictured flow
While yet concealed its barb of woe ;—
Scarce parted we when tidings came
Which scaled my lips o'er one dear name,
And through my three-fold mourning weeds,
My spirit rose to higher deeds,

And life was duty. Then again
Allured by love, I found but pain;
My heart pursuing ideal light,
Became involved in thorny night;
Groping for friendship pure as mine,
Another's hate became its shrine;
But I, my own possessing still,
Escaped that blind, perverted will;
Disfranchised, wandered o'er the Earth,
To find—true love's untainted worth.'

Again he speaks : 'Wilt thou resign
All other hopes of love for mine ;
Let thy sweet soul embrace my own,
The last, the nearest—only one —
In all the future, good or ill,
Who may thy dreams of love fulfil ?
Love thrives in lone and desert air,
When God and truth unite the pair ;
And in this wilderness may we
Grow strong in its felicity ;
Here bind and feel the purest joy
The world may know, freed from alloy
Of fashion's strife, or envy's sighs,
The jewel happiness our prize !'

'If I my own fond heart do know,
Too happy be its impulse now,
Loving but thee. 'Tis like a fount
Long sealed within a shaded mount,

O'er which has moved thy magic hand,
And bursting forth at its command,
The tide must evermore for thee
Flow gently on, instinctively !
    Persuaded now, I love thee more
Than all my heart has asked before ;
Sweet friend, I claim but time to prove
The full devotion of my love !'
When souls are blended, angels smile,
And Earth's great heart is glad the while :
The bright material mother keeps
Her loving watch, nor ever sleeps
When arms long kept from one embrace
Are years in finding the one place
Each pair may twine :— And now she binds
Round these clasped forms and mingled minds
A halo of approval, fair
As aught that in the planet's air
May glow in beauty, though unseen,
Save to those eyes that look between
The spirit's infinite and sense ;
Who see with vision pure, intense,
Through bands that to some souls must be
Ever a spirit mystery.

And we perchance look on this scene
With eyes too rude, though not, I ween,
With dull emotion.   Have we loved ?
Have we the world's elixir proved ?

And be our verdict like the mass
Who 'love,' but fail to keep just pace
With love's fast ripening fruits? What task!—
All credulous—whom do we ask
Now for the wealthy estimate
Of love that never bled to hate,
Or faded to indifference?
Who for the weight of love's suspense
Ere yet its tale was fully told,
Whose balance never rose with gold?

    Vain questions! Each tried heart
Beating its own o'erwearied part,
Has known or yet may know the strain
Of such experimental pain;
Transporting pathos of warm thought
Which with each nerve of feeling wrought,
Imparts to its elected one
The fervor it will ne'er disown.

A few glad months have changed the scene—
We sing the bridal of Allien;
Winter, with snowy footstep, bore
Diurnal treasures to the shore
Of time   departed; warming gleams
Built castles for the Summer's dreams,
And Spring smiles newly on the tide
Of life and all its worthy pride:
Brighter the month of roses shines,
Edging with gold the forest pines,

Than all before,
To her whose centered soul has found
The heart with her's by nature bound,
    Love asking all no more!
The rich, vast earth no treasure. holds
So precious as the silken folds
    Her raptuous fancy binds;—
O, ardency, complete, serene!
So perfect it hath rarely been,—
    Union of hearts and minds.

That pensive orb which long ago
Bathed Eden with its evening glow;
Whose hallowing lusters all divine,
With time grow holy, softer shine,
Gives the only pearls to her braided hair,
    Silvering the wreath of evergreen
    That, bathed in moonlight, crowns Allien.
No orange-bloom or fabric rare,—
No woven vail sustains the charm
Around her slender graceful form;
No fair attendants strew with flowers
The pathway of the nuptial hours:
Her 'maids' are but the zephyr's wings,—
All hushed her heart's past murmurings;
Her sweet soft cheeks are calm and pale;
Her bright eyes shine from lids too frail;
Her lips are tinted with the dyes

Azaleas* wear 'neath April skies:
Few friends are gathered round the pair
Whose lives are one united prayer;
'Tis love's most simple festival,
Where words of Christian kindness fall
From hearts to sacrifice resigned,—
The gentle and the soul-refined,
Whose inner beings almost know
The Savior's, sacrificial woe!

And moving there, an unseen one
Bears on her spirit-head a crown
Of Eden's amaranthine gems,
Richer than queenly diadems:
A harp of silver strings she keeps,
And that fair bride's sweet soul she steeps
In blissful music! What her name?
Alas! 'tis known to pride, and fame,
To wealth, and honor, and to hate,—
To all desires life may create;
But never stained by all or one,
HOPE is the soul's unsetting sun,
Attendant meet for such a scene,—
The angel - sister of Allien!

And mingled there a darker form,
With eye subdued like a dying storm,

---

* The Azalea nudiflora of Linnæus is a beautiful species of Rhododendron, growing in the woods of Eastern and Central New York, profusely flowering in April, before the leaves are half-grown, very fragrant, large, in clusters; their hue a soft, indescribable rose-pink.

With silent lips and mien of pride,
Watching the fair and pensive bride:
He moved like one who lives apart,
In the silence of his own deep heart,
Expressive only to his race,
Rebuking feeling's sunny trace,
And all those nameless arts that move
Another to a thought of love :—
Curbing a voice that rarely gave
Its solemn bass to accents grave,
He looked as though no barrier stood
Before his sight, no fleshly hood
Repelled his inner gaze of light,
Beyond the wall of mortal night.

Ontara's gift was the only one
Bestowed without a smile or tone,—
A cross his own rude hands had made,
Smoothly with painted quills inlaid,—
A hollow cross, with cubic throat,
And fringed with beads in pearly rote,
Wherein in white profusion stood
Rare blossoms from a distant wood.

She took the offering from one
Whose inward life, like hers, had grown,
Bowing in that sequestered place,
With all the charm of courtly grace:
Then, slowly, like the wane of day,
The prophet turned and went his way.

Complacent, leave the once succeeding years,
Their energies and changes, happiness and tears,]
Written more clear in volumes of the past,
Sealed to eternity : some page, the last,
Must bring us to the tale's material close,—
O, soft in favoring minds be its repose !
If one should, flattering, wish the record more,
I point him to the Infinite's far shore,
Where open every history shall be
To one eternal judgment's just decree.
The lips that told to me, in death are still—
Lives none who such request might now fulfill.

Not strange, methinks, the course that pair defined,
Though brief in union life's career, designed
By Heaven ; duty's inward imprints asking,
Each day, though to perform were overtasking ;
They lived, they toiled, they suffered, blessed and loved,
They laid them down in peace when God removed
His lent spark immortal,—all was done,—
The pure disfranchised soul death's victory won.

Ah ! sum so little, signs so faint of all
Mankind may, from the cradle to the pall,
Produce, fill up, describe and solve in part,—
Is this—rude tale—the story of a heart?
Of one. And from the Omniscient's gracious throne
Hope brings a promise that He deigns to own
Its simple record one approving scene
In th' unwritten drama of the 'Might have been.'

Weep not for those who die in Summer's prime,
Whose beauty fades ere noonday's silvery chime;
Who pass serenely from their labors here,
Reliant on the future, whom no tear
Of vain regret betrays life's purpose failed;
Whose true devotion, grief left unassailed
Rejoice that mortal sorrows, strife and cloud,
On such lives wasted like a snow-flake shroud
From vernal bloom; that virtue's placid reign
Was not dispelled by disappointment's pain.

Dear reader, such was she whose being kept
Its own chaste sanctity, from which there crept
No secret staining shadow, no distrust
Of man or God, believing nature just;
Whose aims were self-possessed, content, complete,
Heroic, hopeful, loving.   We have seen
The gentle childhood of the pure Allien:
The roses of her youth before us smiled,—
Not rare exotics, not e'en blossoms wild
Of pastures, prairies, woods, or ruins damp,
Deserted garden, or of poisonous swamp,
But virtues cultured by the careful hands
Of parents strong in duty's stern commands:
And, too, we saw the dews of girlhood's love,
Ere yet her heart of its own will would rove,
Distill upon its fair parterre, and shine
In radiance no iris may combine;

Love's offered fervor, with youth's guileless art,
Kindled the sleeping raptures of her heart,
And life was bliss.

       *   *   *   *   *   *

                      The sorrowing climax came,
And 'Oscar' lived—a sweet unuttered name,
A memory, a hope of Heaven :—then life
Seemed but a monitor of duty's strife ;
Affection's triple-woven chain was broken,
But warm from stranger hearts new love was spoken ;
The youthful orphan found, in earth's rude wild,
Bright skies above 'neath which the flowers still smiled,
And by her own sweet truth, the star
Of morning crowned this shaded tiara.
 First love to her was nature's gushing tide
Of pure affection, lost, so never tried
By love's deep, mastering passion, spirit-asking
Granted to souls but once, or never:—Death unmasking
While it wounded, proved the agency
Of more intense felicity ;
And through this full insphering of its power,
She saw a fallacy, re-named the flower,—
Christened anew the dead, a 'brother' lost ;—
One dream grew dimmer, this was all the cost.

We may not dwell on life's last closing scene,
But, gentle reader, give our lost Allien—
A sigh ? A tear ? A song ?—Ah, no, a smile,

. A pledge of hope.—Upon a cedar isle,
Near Upper Mississippi's pebbly shore,
Her ashes rest ; her sweet soul evermore
Rejoices in the Eden of the skies,
A song-bird of the Savior's Paradise.

REFRAIN.

Grand River !   Flowing ever **on**
    Murmur approval now :
Thy rippling inspiration gone,
    Frowns gathering on thy brow,
Denied the smiles of thy wide vale,
And who could weave another tale?

Imperial waters of the West,
    Circlet of many a clime,
Long be each coronet and crest
    Tribute to thee and time ;
Posterity applaud forever
Thy use and beauty, stately River !

Beneficent thy ministries
Millions of graves declare :
Sons wandering far 'neath foreign skies,
And red men native there,
Vanquished by death, from year to year,
Time immemorial claim thy tear !

How long?—The wilderness is dark—
Thought's unanswering domain :—
How long !—Is there response?—Peace, hark !
How long shall be thy reign?
Ask God man's fate in His decrees,
But check inquiries vague as these !

Reluctant, turn, my muse, away ;
Farewell, grand sovereign tide !
What though I wander many a day,—
Remembrance fosters pride ;
And when I roam thy banks again,
I still may dream of fair Allien !

MISCELLANEOUS POEMS.

HAPPINESS AND INDUSTRY.

'Happy, happy,' on the mountain,
　　Seemed to think a blue hair-bell,—
　　'I've no tale of grief to tell :'—
'Happy always,' spoke a fountain,
　　As its gushing waters fell
　　In a marble chisseled well.

'I am happy,' looked a daisy,
　　On the meadow's emerald bed,
　　Blooming with the clover red :—
'Happy in the dances mazy,'—
　　Thus a youthful maiden said,
　　Tossing gay her curly head.

'Happy, happy,' drone-bees murmur,—
　　'Riches — sweets of industry—
　　Hoarded in the hive I see :'—
'Happy in the golden Summer,—
　　It has flowers and fruits for me,'
　　Sang a youth all merrily.

9　　　　　　　　　　　　　M

Blooms may nod in idle beauty ;
  Waters rest in sparkling pride ;
  Queen-bees, drones, in honey hide :
Manhood has a path of duty
  Spread before it clear and wide ;
  Turn, O turn not it aside !

Yes—contentment is a treasure !
  Seek it for its priceless worth,
  It is rare upon the earth ;—
Not like drones enjoy your pleasure,—
  Fields uncultured cause a dearth,—
  Idleness is sterile mirth.

Parasitic, torrid verdure,
  All with grace and beauty rife—
  Other rootings give it life !
Whoso has no self-earned larder
  Has no meed of noble strife,
  Living but a crippled life.

REMEMBRANCES.

Like pictures bright they sometimes gleam
  Along our present way ;—
Like bell-tones lost, or wasted stream,
  They pass, and where are they?
They show us oft and oft again,
  Youth's glory-beaming morn ;—
Since then we've learned the spirit's pain,
  When hope breathed low and care was born!

And memory stands a spectral friend,
  To fan affection's fire,
When light and shade unequal blend,
  And trembling hopes expire
Beneath that star whose lofty ray
  Scarce greets the heart's deep well,
Eternal Faith, for which we pray,
  Sin's tumults wild to quell.

MORNING IN THE COUNTRY.

The fair invigorated earth
    From Night's embrace awakes ;
Iris in all its myriad birth
    From every dew-gem breaks,
While from th' uncurtained orient streams
    Apollo's radiating beams !

Opals and diamonds glitter bright,
    On blade and leaf and flower,
As though the condescending night
    Had given her stars for dower,
And Beauty in their rich array
Became the bride of royal Day !

Voices attuned to Nature's song
    Creation's joys declare ;
Music's unfettered, guileless throng
    Control the powers of air,
And harmonies mysterious swell
From wood to wood, from plain to dell !

Ah, Peace ! Thou hast a peerless throne,
   A canopy, a shrine,
Where woodlands old, and prairies, own
   Their regions realms of thine,
Whose pure elixirs offer balm
To every heart that needeth calm !

Lives there a soul whose sense of life
   No morning has imbued
With hearty scorn of gold, and strife
   Of forum, field and feud,
Unblessing God that he was born,
While drinking from the cup of morn !

EVENING IN THE COUNTRY.

I've watched from noon to wane of day,
  A fleet of white clouds sail
Along yon broad cerulean way,
  Soft, silvery and frail ;
And now they rally in the west,
Seeking a dreamy port of rest.

Bright navy of the vaulted sky !
  Who guides your courses there ?
Who spread your fleecy sails so high
  To furl in evening air ?
Unlike too many lovely forms,
Ye glow the brighter after storms !

As sinks the day they're growing dim ;—
  Sweet sounds are dying slow ;—
The horizon's far wavy rim
  Bounds no vast peaks of snow,
But, 'Alp on Alp,' in ether stand,
Grey, solemn sentinels and grand !

Now on the verdant thirsty soil
  Distilling dew descends ;
And rest—sweet visitant of toil—
  Each weary form befriends ;
And Nature's harp, though hushed its lays,
Still trembles with its Maker's praise.

As dies its murmurs near and far,
  Immortal longings thrill
The soul, which chafes its fleshly bar
  To scape material ill,
That Heaven and Peace may seal its bliss
In hours more hallowing than this.

The day has wandered, felt, unseen,
  To memory's laureled land,
Whose chaplets fair—forever green,
  Array its shadowy band,
Who wait time's mandate to restore—
Waiting in vain—the days of yore.

THE CHILDREN OF ÆOLUS.

Where spreads a vast etherial stream,
    Translucent as the eye of morn,
In realms of air where sapphires gleam,
    And amethysts the domes adorn,—
Where noiseless clouds in dreamy dance
    Arise invisible from earth,
Surrounded by a dark expanse,
    The winds, the wondrous winds, have birth.

They linger not in native halls,—
    Their viewless wings impulsive swell;
Anon, the breeze of evening calls
    With whispers through a leafy dell :—
It glides within a cottage door,
    Bends down to kiss an infant's curls,
Then lightly sweeps the sanded floor,
    And with the snowy curtain twirls.

'Tis gone !   The gathering shades of night
    Impel the cottagers to rest;

A sparkling wreath of astral light
    Sublimely circles midnight's crest;—
The calm is brief,—a power 's abroad,
    Whose rising voice proclaims its sway;
The fierce north-wind is shrieking loud,
    And Nature's forms are in dismay.

Glad morning sunbeams smile again,
    Sweet sounds arise from feathered throngs,
Fair Flora and her laughing train
    Dispense rich bloom and witching songs;
From man creation's anthem swells;
    No winds disturb the opening day,
But where the ocean laves its shells,
    They're tossing many a gem of spray.

The east wind seeks dim Tartar plains,
    Arabia's sandy, spicy woods,
The crumbling shrines fair Greece retains,
    The Delta's bounteous, sacred floods:
It sometimes travels o'er the sea
    When Oriental sails unfurled
Waft treasures to some foreign lea,
    From many a palmy island world.

The west wind loves the Alpine cloud,
    Divides the Avalanche's seam,
Lays on the Switzer's cot a shroud,
    Binds crystal ripples on the stream:

It visits Summer in disguise,—
   'Mong softly stirring, listless leaves,
It bids the resting pilgrim rise,
   Ere yet the storm a tumult weaves.

These formless children of the sky,
   Eccentric in their loves, desire
Pledges of no fraternal tie,
   Of no Promethean fire.
With ease they revel in the sphere
   Created for responsive man;
And when the rainbow sheds its tear,
   The winds subdued, its beauties scan.

ANALOGY.

Flowers by the wayside,
  Scattered here and there ;
See them by the river's tide
  Growing sweet and fair !
Flowers on the mountain,
Blossoms by the fountain,
Violets in the wildwood,
Daisies, loved of childhood,
Hollyhock and golden-rod,
Buttercups where paths are trod,
  How they will in manhood grown
  Make a slumbering memory known?

Words of pleasant kindness
  Springing from the heart,
Waking hope from blindness
  Healing sorrow's smart,
Gracious human flowers
From affection's bowers,
Blooms not soon to perish,
Charmers grief may cherish,
Shining round the portal
Of a mind immortal,—
  If you 've nothing else to give,
  Oh ! bestow them while you live !

SUNSET QUESTIONS.

O, what in this calm hour of Nature's sweetness
    Disturbs my inward rest,
With such a burdening sense of incompleteness
    I know not how to test?
Look I for beauty, outward form and feature,
    Serene beyond compare?
Lovely inanimation, image, creature,—
    Sublimity more rare?
Waits my faint soul for music's new entrancement,
    For harmonies ideal ;
For this celestial power's up-winged advancement,—
    Strophes divine, unreal?
Listens my thought, an echoing discerner
    Of memories of the past,—
A statue, waiting time's inbreathed sojourner,
    To make its outlines last?
Am I of Earth or mortal agents asking
    Some happiness denied,
Or e'en imploring Heaven, overtasking
    Soul-strength before untried?
Love, poesy, religion, O, relieve me !
    What doth my heart require?
The half-revealing secret is,—believe me,—
    Love smothering its own fire !

A COMPARISON

When sunlight on a pink-white rose
Grows softer in its gathered dew,
The flower, unconscious why it grows
So sweet, and beauteous in hue,
Is as the picture to us seems   .
When baby smiles amid his dreams.

TO MY FATHER ON HIS SIXTIETH BIRTHDAY.

———

Art thou in thy far mountain home
   Numbering thy vanished years to-day?
Alone do thy slow footsteps roam,
   To ponder on thy children's play
In Summer hours departed long,
So like a dying strain of song?

Or there, beneath the cedars grand,
   Bends low thy sad and thoughtful head,
Bestowing on thy native land
   Sighs for its peace and glory dead,
The dull red glimmer of its shield,—
Mistaken honor of the field !

Dear father, almost loth am I
   To count the shadows of thy years ;
And O, I cannot tell thee why,
   A seal is on the fount of tears !
But feeling, like the ocean deep,
A calm exterior may keep.

Three-score! The cycles, one by one,
  Have left faint impress on thy face :—
Fancy wings back to childhood gone,
  But no forgetting can erase
Lines of dull care and curves of thought,
By time's unresting pencils wrought.

To-day I'd rove that vale with thee,
  Would breathe its pure elixir air;
My heart so bounding when 'tis free
  Nature's wild harmonies to share,
Would almost back to infancy
To rest upon thy parent knee!

But tell me not of radiant bloom
  Beneath the 'summit's' snowy band;
My soul so longs once there to roam
  On grass that springs from golden sand,
Where meeting seasons blend their charms
And Summer smiles in Winter's arms!

The future gives no promise yet,
  And I must leave thee, father, still
Almost alone, thy mild eyes wet
  With tears from fond affection's rill :
But God is round thee; by his care
Thy days shall move as safely there!

O, BURY ME IN SOME FOREST GRAND.

O, bury me in some forest grand,
    Beneath an aged sheltering tree,
In the soil of my own dear native land,
    Where all things are so fair and free !
In a wild-wood deep where sound the chords
    By unseen fingers strangely played,
To charm proud Nature's silent lords
    With spheral song and serenade :—
O, bury me there ;—I'd die in Spring,
    In dasied May, or rose-sweet June ,
When every heart so longs to sing,
    Responsive to high Nature's tune :
When smile the loves of Flora's train
    At the feet of branching monarchs old,
And fringy robes of sea-green pines
    Give brighter tinge from every fold !
I'd rather rest where untrimmed boughs
    Weave laceries above my head,
Than sleep where Caria's queen bestows
    The costliest structure for her dead !
But O, I'd have a loving friend
    Kneel sometimes by my lonely tomb,
On whom my spirit might descend,
    Winning unseen to love's bright home !

THE DEATH OF SUMMER.

The airs of mild retreating hours
  In soft embracings float around,
While pensively maturing flowers
  Lean toward the silent, somber ground:
From Nature's mist-enveloped lyre
  Symphonic sweetness trembles low;
A faded hue its vestures wear,—
  Funereal murmurs come and go.

To-day, the last of Summer days,
  Old Time recalls the season's breath;
But so to sympathize displays
  Banners of promise for its death:—
To-morrow's sun will gild a bier,
  Where lies in pageant state a queen,
So late the monarch of the year
  Her foot-prints guide her burial-train.

Let grains of gold be scattered o'er
  The parted Summer's flower-lined tomb,

And fruits delicious, which she bore
From blossoms legacied of June;
And spread no dark portentous pall
Around her vanquished loveliness,
But leaves she nourished, in their fall,
Weave crimson folds her bier to dress.

November's plaintive breezes sing
A triumph-dirge, O queen, for you,
When birds have flown on startled wing,
Where Summer lives as though anew!
Yon sinking sun, cloud-marshaling,
Let fall those many-colored gems
For kindred muses thence to string
The *nonpareil* of diadems!

LOST TREASURES.

When Spring's soft skies were silver-blue,
I nursed a flower of gentle hue ;
When life and love, and hope's gay train
Broke forth anew with joy's glad strain :—
My blossom owned a fragrant heart,
And envying bees would near it dart ;—
It was not white nor red, but just
A hue between, and when 't was brushed
'Neath Venus' smile with evening dew,
'T was the richest bloom I ever knew :
Its beauty with each dream of mine,
In vain delight I sought to twine ;—
Alas ! one morn a growing wind
Told me my gentle thing to find ;—
Gone was its fashion,— scattered far
Its folds of waxy petals were !
I asked the breezes where they fell,
They moaned again, but would not tell ;
Then pensively I walked away,

My rose-queen mourning all that day.

*　　*　　*　　*　　*　　*

Time passed along, another flower
Just from a far immortal bower,
Mysterious drew my doting heart!
It too was beauty's partial part,
For it eclipsed the galaxy
Of garden and conservatory :—
A mind illumed the precious form,—
A soul, sent forth by the 'I Am!'
In ecstacy of love and deep,
This prize I surely thought to keep,
And guarded it with hourly care,
While sweet it breathed of Heaven's air:
But, ah! as once before, it came
My proud and selfish heart to tame;
For soon with wings of light it flew
To grander life beyond the blue;
And now I love the humblest flowers,—
Dim, way-side plants of stinted dowers.

THE SPIRIT OF BEAUTY.

The spirit of beauty reigns everywhere,
Pervading the earth, the ocean, and air;
With wisdom divine its empire began,—
Creation of God and treasure of man :—
Its breath is the south-wind's lulling note ;
On the azure of noontide its winglets float ;
Its drapery curtains the sun to rest
In the mystic chamber of the rainbow-west :
It sings when storm has left the sea,—
Its voice is known in the murmuring bee ;
In bowers of verdure its music is heard,
When carols in joy the innocent bird :
Its children are leaves and sunbeams and flowers,
Its companions the soft invisible hours ;—
It loves not a part but all of the earth,
For where do not beauteous things have birth !
    Where man has ne'er trod, in ocean-bound caves,
It fashions bright shells to sing with the waves,
And sends the fair nautilus on the seas,
To sail o'er the waters with natural ease :

It shines in gems of the earth and the deep,
In the soft-falling snow, in the glacier's wild sweep,
And it breaks the gloom of the Arctic night
With the brilliant Aurora's wondrous light:
It sleeps in the folded shades of even
Or rests in the starry calm of Heaven;
Its food is immortal — the essence of love;
The spirit of beauty is nourished above!

A DREAM.

I walked the shaded village green,
  Passed by the old church door,
Entered the school-house brown again,
  Sat by my desk once more :

I heard the hasty morning bell,—
  A careless throng came in;
The master's voice essayed to quell
  And hush the deafening din :

Then as of old he slowly read
  From books the best of all,
And solemn prayer went forth that led
  The mind from bat and ball.

The sun advanced, the lessons learned,
  More restless were the crowd,
Till out again they all were turned,
  With whoop and halloo loud !

Then scampering on o'er clover meads,
  Disporting to each home,
Some stopped for flowers, or pebble beads,
  Beside the cascade's foam.

And as diverse their paths appeared
  Life's later paths have run ;—
So my brief vision disappeared
  Before the present's sun.

10

TO A FRIEND OF THE PAST.

Dear Rachel mine, I'd trace a lay
   With love's pure images inwrought.
O'er which thine eyes may fondly stray
   With impulse of impassioned thought!

I'd touch a heart to memory dear,
   The soft Æolian of the mind,
Whose subtle strings can scarce appear,
   For time hath made them undefined!

Come from thine unknown love-haunt now
   And with my distant spirit feel
That potent charm, our early vow,
   Which fancy folds its wings to seal!

Again with careless feet we're straying
   Through dreamy vistas of the past;
Before our morning life-shrines laying
   Affection's offering, cloud-o'ercast!

Again we smile where 'Oakley' smiles
O'er Hudson's peaceful island tide,
Whose mirroring breast the sky beguiles
To give its azure for his bride !

And this was HOME, the heart's content,
Sacred to peace — though justice long
Withheld approval — where we spent
Delightful days of love and song !

There oft thy sweet guitar and free
Its pensive, tinkling numbers woke
While plaintive words etherially
From thy soft accents broke !

How deeply then I longed to sing,
To mingle with thy flowing strain,
And mount as on the spirit's wing ;—
For vocal song I sighed in vain !

I must not linger here with thee,
Else from my restless inward life
May burst a stream to swell the sea
Of sorrow's overwhelming strife !

RAYS OF LIGHT.

See them through the darkness gleaming
　　See them edging every cloud !
O behold them softly streaming
　　O'er the throng of patriots bowed
'Neath the banner of the stars,
Resting from the UNION's wars !

Now the shadows shift their changes,
　　Aureate the folds become ;
Brothers,—freemen,—friends and strangers
　　Gather, joyful as they come,·
Swelling pæans, sounding royal
Diapasons of the loyal !

Wider, stronger grow the beamings,
　　More cerulean shines the sky,
More beneficent the dreamings
　　Of the soul of Liberty :
Peace, white winged, has left her eyrie.
Rescued from her vigil dreary !

And the eagles,—see their pinions
Hasting downward through the air,—
Scanning all the broad dominions
Of a region rich and fair !
Ah ! they perch upon the altar
Round which heroes never falter !

Now upon this shrine of glory
Justice showers laurels green,
While she stamps the thrilling story
Of new struggles that have been,
When the noblest souls were banded,
Unrelenting, iron-handed !

Sun of Freedom ! Thou art shining,
Unbeclouded is thy blaze,
Memory's midnight interlining,
Hallowing dim departed days,
On Progression's standard high
Fixing every patriot's eye !

November, 1861.

RETROSPECTION.

These Autumn airs that kiss my brow and sigh for
    Summer's youth,
Bear on their violet winglets incense of the heart's
    deep truth :—
Afar the years have wandered since that sad consol-
    ing hour :
The Springs have bloomed, and died the bright Au-
    tumnal flower.
The angel of my being smiled upon a mournful path,
For I'm an orphan ;—life was darkened by my pa-
    rents' death.

One gentle day like this, I wandered forth alone, to
    kneel
Upon the leaf-strewn mound, in grief which none but
    orphan's feel ;
The golden-rods moved lightly in the cool and scented
    breeze,
And all the forms of nature vied the intellect
    please ;

A crown of gold and purple rested on the distant hills
Adown their sunny sides like silver flowed the joy
 ous rills ;
I sat upon the double grave, and mused on grief and
 death,
When something stirred the boughs more strong than
 stirred the zephyr's breath ;—
A stranger stood before me—one with proud and
 noble form,—
His gracious words fell softly, for his heart was kind
 and warm :—

*   *   *   *   *   *

Time passed away, and from that holy hour I learned
 to love ;
While resting on his breast I saw the angels smile
 above !
The void of my lone heart grew fruitful of a pure
 delight ;
My soul, no more desponding, saw no more a starless
 night ;
My palpable existence seemed no more a shattered
 shroud ;
A halo shown around like rays that glorify the cloud
And beauty all-pervading fed my longing mind again
So nought in all the world semed dark or sorrowful,
 or vain !
Then duty called my precious one,—he wandered oe'r
 the sea ;—

Our spirits parted not, nor will in God's eternity.
How trustingly I waited, but his form came back no
    more !
He landed on the unexplored, far-off, immortal shore ;
And patiently I wait for closer union in that clime
Where no decay sheds darkness on the sun-lit track
    of time.

UNREST.

What do I ask in this uncertain hour?
My over-anxious heart
Shrinks like the inner petals of a flower,
Full blown, its counterpart,—
O not a blossom rare, but free and wild,—
Dweller of shaded dell, or mountain child!

Is there a fount of joy in inward song?
Do I claim a fuller tide?
Quaffing alone, am I than once less strong
In faith, in love, or pride?
What do these undefined murmurs ask—
Has duty or content become a task?

Does slumbering energy complain
Its wasting nerve unused?
Why congregate these clouds, portending rain—
O why these eyes suffused
With herald tears?—This must be transient grief!
E'en Spring may sometimes drop a 'yellow leaf.'

Faint heart! Thou hast a faithful sentinel,—
Unvail to Hope thine eyes;
She guards thy longing dreams of love so well,
Before thee to the skies
Their beauty shall pass on;—how sweetly there
Thou yet mayst breathe in pure affection's air!

10*   o

INSPIRATION.

———

Breezes of Autumn, whence your wandering wings,
    Bearing sweet balm to my inquiring soul!
From what rich land.vibrate your viewless strings?
    Where shines the sea to which your currents roll?—
This dreamy mood your spirit-kiss inspires,—
    This mild forgetfulness of pain and strife,
It soothes my being with refined desires,
    And adds a rainbow charm to love and life.

Spirits of truth and destiny—they come—
    These whisperings of the wild, untrammeled air,
Breathing of an immortal, glorious home,
    Where love and holiness forget despair;
Their influence turns the tide of gloomy thought,
    Melting the heart to bliss;—its mountain snows
Flow downward, to its emerald valleys brought
    In sunny rills, they greet the blooming rose!

Bright Amaranth, whose purple cheeks maintain
  Such royal beauty, whence *thy* lulling power?
Hath this soft wind from Eden's gorgeous plain
  Bequeathed thy magic, rich unfading flower?
And is my heart like thee—its faithful light
  Of sanguine love to burn and glow forever,
Unpaled by disappointment's troubled night,—
  Gilding every shadow, withering never?

Reality! The ideal makes the real,
  The thought that stamps each virgin page of time
And he whose life is patient, earnest, *leal*
  May gather hopes in fruits of life sublime!
Then whisper, gentle airs, instruct my soul,—
  Wisdom and exaltation to it bear;
And when the stream of death shall round me roll,
  I may to God my grateful love declare.

THE SOWING OF LIGHT.

It cometh not in liquid showers,
　　With music murmuring,
Nor as the slow-unfolding flowers
　　Of each returning Spring ;
Not as the tribune of the storm,
　　Nor rippling waters' swell,
Nor lightning blazes of alarm,
　　Nor aught these may dispel.

'T is 'sown' in white and sea-wide streams
　　Falling direct from Heaven ;—
Love's mellowing of its own beams,
　　By truth and beauty given ;
Its harvest ripening all the year,—
　　Its blossoms peace and smiles,—
The fruit Jehovah makes it bear
　　Cheers Earth and all her isles.

It paints all nature in all hues,
  Enchantingly arrayed,
And dungeon airs it may infuse
  From color's gay arcade ;
It brings the morn to fever's pain,
  And day's rebuke to crime,
And carves the amethystine vein
  That makes the mount sublime.

It tints the infant's open eyes,
  And shows the grave-shroud pure,
And, lingering, lets the evening skies
  The lover's steps allure ;—
The painter's art is scarce his own,—
  In fractions of the hours
Light on the *camera* is sown,
  And eyes we love are ours.

MY STARS.

Blue eyes, bright eyes,
Let your sunrise
Open my lids to smile,
My sorrowing dream exile,
This parting reconcile,
And bid me hope nor longer weep,—
In love's dew-bloom my sad soul steep,
And let me feel anew
Such light is ever true!

Fond eyes, loved eyes,
Which otherwise
Have never looked on me,
Though wandering far, still see
The need mine have of ye,—
Still be their tender substitute,
And may no foreign ones compute
The bliss you thus discover,
Brightening *our* world all over!

Pure eyes, proud eyes,
God's mysteries !
Teach me as oft before,
With your enchanting lore,
To worship more and more
Beauty and intellect divine,
Trembling. beside its mortal shrine
In rays so manifest,
Making me more than blest !

Kind eyes, thought eyes,
Sweet, silent.sighs,
A wealth of peace conveying
When misery surveying,—
Potential faith's calm praying,—
Half shade your partial brightness now,
While deepening inward, knowing how
One sits alone, alone,
Singing love's monotone !

O gentle eyes !
Ye sympathize,
And, spirit-borne, compel
Me yet again to tell
I thought not stars could dwell
'Neath human brows in miniature,
Lessening joy's distance to insure
Perpetual delight,—
Rare jewels of my night !

MY COMPANION.

Spirit of Solitude, reflection's queen,
Majestic in thy loneliness serene—
Beneficent in all thy ministry,
Though unconfest by those who silently
Bemoan their contradicting destiny,—
Thou art my cherished friend; and yet to tell
Another how 'tis so serves to dispel
His cheery smile, or make a gay heart shun
The chamber of the melancholy one!
So thou to me art not a phantom grim—
A discord in my life's low murmured hymn,
Nor verdict of forgetfulness of joy,
Rebuking not, though on a toy
Occasion lets me look and sometimes smile;
Nor frowning when wild birds and flowers beguile
My mood from contemplation more sublime,
When thought, a vine, is not a vine to climb!

I love thee, watchful and exclusive one;
Favored by thee, I need not feel alone!

Disclose thy confidence—a sorceress
Is but the child of fable,—I possess
Her magic, vivified with ecstacy
All real and present, when I summon thee,
A willing though a casual visitor,
And draw the curtains round my inner door!
Then—no, I'll not tell all the world, nor part,
How soothing and encouraging thou art;
How beautiful and solemn is the story
We then together read; thou with thy hoary,
Grand, consecrated head, so wise, yet mild,
And I beside thee, learning like a child!

FANTASIE.

———

Once from a darkly vaulted cave
  Some prisoned waters broke,
And hasted forward brightly brave,
  For they to light awoke.

A brooklet cheery, on it went
  Through wild-woods deep and vast,
Where ferns and flowers o'er it bent
  And graceful figures cast.

And on—meandering through the vales
  Where lilies waved in pride,
And falling petals mimic gales
  Snowed softly on its tide;

Where splendid sunbeams grandly smiled
  On ripples to it born,
As laving rocky feet more wild
  Its narrowed course led on.

Blue ocean's broad, unfathomed deep
  Received its child at length,
And though absorbed, it loves to sleep
  Within creative strength.

And so the soul—man's deathless mind,
  By thought's Eternal given,
Rolls onward till its currents find
  An ocean rest in Heaven.

DISTRUST.

I saw a squirrel nimbly bound
  In graceful shyness on the hill,
His eyes surveying all the ground
  In search of food his mouth to fill.

With step abated, I advanced
  That I the sprite might plainer see ;—
Ah, ha ! provokingly he danced,
  And darted up our tall pine tree !

'Come down,' in accents mild I said,
  'I'd never do a squirrel harm ;
I'll smooth your fur, and give you food,
  And nest of down all white and warm !'

'Nay, gentle Miss, I would not dare,
  I'm sure, to trust myself with you,
For something says, "take care, take care,"
  You might to squirrel prove untrue.

I could not bide a gilded cage,
　　Were it the finest ever seen ;
Nor ever learn your maxims sage,—
　　A free-born native of the green !

'So if you'll please to walk away,
　　I'll scamper to my hidden home ;
And when you'd visit Squirrel Grey,
　　Just sound the woods and I will come.

'Bounding before your footsteps then,
　　I'll lead where rarest blossoms grow ;—
In wild-wood deep, and mossy glen,
　　I'll show you where blue viols blow !'

I turned, and quick he fled my sight,
　　As thoughts of beauty sometimes fly;—
I almost wept behind his flight,
　　And deemed him happier than L

SECRET LIFE.

Contrasting often ;—each one hath
   Two spheres, the inner not the mate
   Of the creation visible to all ;
Two forms pursue one being's path ;
   Two natures for the last change wait,—
   Duality, ideal and literal !

Mysterious Realm ! Philosophy
   Is proud to gain its ivied portals,
     And write for truth on its exclusive page
Time's silent tales. Mild history
   Sighs, incomplete, for those immortals,
     Thoughts and emotions for her ken too sage.

Love owns alone the certain key,
　　Which fate forbids a frequent using,
　　　　And death, disturbing, weakens its weird power:
Ripple, and swell, and wave, we see,
　　And storm we feel, and joy's diffusing,
　　　　Of that dear life we love, but what its dower ?

The gift of insight to its strife
　　Of impulse silenced, sin repelled ;
　　　　Of hope's allurings gently questioned. wisely ;
Of all the spirit wealth of life,
　　Decay subverted, dross expelled,-
　　　　Duty's interior balance poised precisely !

THE SPIRIT OF SPRING.

Like a white sea-bird, over time's deep wave
  An angel comes with glory intense,
  Whose wings will rest in foliage dense
When clovers are purpling on the Winter's dim grave.

Tis the gentle Spring from her home above,—
  Her sweet blue eye is moist with a tear,
  A stranger there for many a year,
Sparkling with thought and pitying love.

Can ye tell who strive for your country now,—
  Brave freemen strong in Heaven and right!
  Ye mourners bowing amid the wild night,—
Can ye answer why this fountain should flow?

Are we told that sorrow is tearless and stern,
  When deep and true, eternal and strong;
  That weeping eyes grow brilliant in song
When the lamps of hope for new pleasures burn?

But the Spring is mourning for this land of ours,
  Red stained with blood its brothers have shed;
  Her voice is prayer for the living and dead,—
She would crown them all with her beautiful flowers.

And rainbows wreathing her forehead of truth
  Shall only fade in victory's sun,
  When Freedom's arms new glories have won
To perpetuate Columbia's youth!

March, 1862.

11

TO AN ABSENT HUSBAND.

When all the world are sleeping,
   When thought is calm and free,
In midnight's hush of beauty,
   My love, I fly to thee!

When stars and airs and waters
   Send forth their angels fair,
To charm the wandering dreamer,
   I'm with thee, dearest, there!

Entranced with spirit-music,
   We ramble through our past,
'Neath shades and hallowed archways,
   'Mid blooms too fair to last.

In paths through meadows winding—
   The emerald plains of bliss—
And on its lofty mountains,
   Where snow and sunbeams kiss.

The morning of our bridal
Dawns on us, dear, once more :
We feel its halcyon promise,
And live it o'er and o'er !

But then grim storm-clouds gather,—
Ay, through the passing years
Their thunders are repeated,
And I awake—in tears.

Tears, not of dark repining,
But joy's and grief's o'erflow,
Commingling in the fountain,
Ere Nature bade them go.

Ah ! then life's holiest angels,
Hope, Faith, and trusting Love,
Around me sing their chorals,
And peace is mine, dear love !

CONTENTMENT.

I live in Ferndell, where my home
   Is carpeted with velvet moss,
And from it never would I roam,
   Nor once my emerald threshold cross
For all the world has sung or smiled,—
I 'm Love's contented, modest child :
                Violet.

My home o'erhangs the precipice
   Time's waves or bolts have cleft asunder,
Where passively I meet the kiss
   Of breezes soft, or shocks of thunder ;
And from the cliff my bloom adorns,
I shower the plain with ruby horns :
              Columbine.

I blossom where warm sunbeams find
   No forest shadows to pervade ;
Where monarch trees have ne'er declined,
   By paths the buffalo have made ;
I love the unobstructed plain,

             Prairie Rose.

Where darkest and most still the aisles
  Of woods' primeval signal time
Where light's gay iris never smiles,
  And hushed is Nature's festal chime,
Owning no tint of green, I fold
My pearl dress near the dead leaves' mould :
                              Monotropa.

I float upon the water's breast,
  Yet far from home I never go ;
Enough for me to be carest
  By Summer airs and tides below ;
To wear robes hued like angels', and
Freight winds with fragrance for the land :
                              Pond Lily.

Where burns the zenith's sun I bloom, —
  Strange, strange to me are fabled showers ;
The thorny wall that guards my home
  Is proud of crested carmine flowers ;
And were I not so strong, and harsh, and rude,
I'd wither in the tropic solitude :
                              Cactus.

FORBIDDEN JOYS.

They come when fancy to the spirit brings
The rapturous touch of her etherial wings,
When all we long for seems within our reach,
But to recede like wavelets on the beach!
They come amid the curtained bloom of dreams,
Gathering like dews from Eden's silver streams,
To flee, alas! as wondrously away
As doth the diamond's phosphorescent ray,—
Sparkling a moment in the deeps of night,
And where, we ask, hath flown our brief delight?
Ah! when thus erringly we seem to feel
Forbidden pleasure, still we sigh, and steal,
Half consciously, scarce knowing if 'tis sin,
Or blessedness that thrills us so within.
O mortal strifes of this embittered state!

Your feverish joys and pains ofttimes create
Harmonious hopes of happiness and love,—
Reflections of serenity above :
And when the wearied, worn, despairing heart,
Enfeebled by suspense, would fain depart
Its mortal bound, O rarely burns anew
The torch of hope, than all before more true;
When love's elastic clasps of tenderness
Entwine with new tenacity of bliss
The idol of affection, and we smile,
And smile again, like sunbeams on an ocean isle.

MURMURS

How long will it be?   How long will it be?
　When my spirit leaves its house of clay,
Will it soar to heaven with time's slow flight,
Or speed like a noiseless ray of light
　To its home eternal far away?

How long will it be?   How long will it be?
　Ere comes the rest of this full release,—
A month or a day, an hour or a year,
Prolonging the fever, the sigh and the tear,—
　Watching the moments in their slow decrease?

How long will it be?　O answer me!
　Revelation, Nature, I ask in vain;
My course on earth—my labor done,—
Have I the mute measure almost run
　To the climax throb, the dying pain?

Ye shadows of gloom, away from me,
　Unvail life's joy, oppress not its breath!
I'll smile though my heart be wasting and worn,
Its sheltering draperies soiled and torn,
　Since the portal of Heaven is entered by death.

Not long shall I struggle and weep to see
　The substance displaced for the shadow pale;
Not long like the flower in Spring-time blown
Shall I wait for something unfound and unknown,
　Fruition will come behind the dark vale.

11*

CONTEMPLATIONS.

Ah! whence, thou wondrous winged thought
   Whose changing visions round me throng!
I've not your highest promise caught,
   But still you leave me love and song,
And lead me forth in flowery fields
   Where skies of purple glory spread,
Inviting rest in shade that yields
   Calm memories of the solemn dead!

The dead in nature—last year's bloom,—
   Its penciled leaf and painted flower;
The fruit that fell before the tomb
   Of Winter claimed the Summer hour;
The chrysalis and butterfly;
   The fallen fringes of the pines
That whispered 'immortality,'—
   Creation's proof of God's designs.

I feel there's life in leaves and grass,
  The insect world my homage claims,
When new to earth Spring sun-fires pass
  I see the cowslip catch its flames ;
The clover-globe of mystic sweet
  Has other, gentler charm for me
Than food for kine—by nature meet—
  Or work-house for the honey-bee.

In these communings thought droops wing,—
  I never mourn that I'm alone
For troops of viewless spirits sing,
  And all-pervading love I own ;
But oft I would such moments share,
  And each ennobling sense I feel,
With those who seem so unaware
  How sweet the blisses they reveal !

THE AUGUST SHOWER.

The dewless skies of morning
    Not long were spread,
When trooping clouds gave warning,
    Darkening o'erhead;
Then cooling airs moved stronger,
    More fragrant seemed,—
The solar king no longer
    Triumphant gleamed:
Soon yellow lights came flashing
    Across the panes,
And thunders loudly crashing
    Their viewless chains,
Ground, roof, and tree, and tower,
    Were flooded o'er,—
A bright mysterious shower—
    Still more, and more.
Anon the stream moved onward
    And onward far;—
Each lingering drop fell downward,
    A tiny star!
Again the sunbeams wreathing
    The arch above
Inspired the grateful breathing,
    'OUR GOD IS LOVE!'

'MIMOSA.'

Yes, such I call thee, friend, but thou
  Art fairer than that plant so rare,
    Whose blooms are drops of gold,
Whose leaves, profuse pale emeralds, know
  Approaching contact through the air,
    And soft their edges fold!

Thy nature is too fine for strife
  Like Earth's, where, cold and dark and rude,
    O'erwhelming sorrows stay;
Too exquisite for real life,—
  Better for thee in solitude
    With one true heart to stray!

And I that chosen one would be,
  Watching each moment lest the wind
    Too harshly greet thy brow;

Guarding each sense so tenderly,
  Whispering so soft and so refined
    That thou no pang could know !

O love is rare—such love as mine,
  Which mist-like finds the inmost cell
    Of feeling, life and thought ;
Joy's faintest thrilling to define,
  Grief's lightest cloudlet to dispel,
    Whose sighs with bliss are fraught !

Then chide me not, e'en though extreme
  Solicitude for thee may crush
    Some violets unseen ;
Their scattering fragrance, like a dream
  Disparting in the morning's blush,
    Leaves memory serene.

LAMENTING.

Alas! some forms grow brighter
  When soon to pass away;—
The radiant crown of Autumn
  Embraces dull decay;
The chrysalis awakens
  With gaily spotted wing,
To make a brief, brief transit
  Beyond the tomb of spring.

The gems that rise o'er fountains
  In mock celestial show,
Dazzle the eye a moment
  And brighten as they go!
The noon-day cloudlet ashen
  Flashes in gold and red,
When evening and high nature
  Apollo's curtains spread.

And hope gives promise ever
  Of glory in its flight;
When trusted most it leaves us
  The blank of sorrow's night;
Yet as a fettered eaglet
  Looks longing toward the sky,
I'm trying, aiming always
  Its eyrie to descry!

A home of lofty beauty
  Above the casual storms
That threaten to demolish
  My charming dream-built forms!
Ah! failing here to find it,
  Shall disappointment's gloom
O'ershadow thought's endeavor,
  And song to sorrow doom!

MEMENTO MORI.

When by thy life's green winding path
  Joy's dearest flowrets grow,
  Its smoothest streamlets flow,
Remember, O remember death!

And when inspired by vernal airs
  Young snow-drops ope their eyes,
  When silver waves the skies,
Remember death for beauty cares!

When Summer sings of love and peace—
  Of Paradise again,
  Of golden wealth of grain,
Be mindful of thy soul's release!

When Autumn's crimson dying leaf
  Falls on thy pensive way
  Fluttering to decay,
Memento Mori! Life is brief!

But mourn thou not when Winter chill
  Bids northern snow-sheets fall;
  Greet the prophetic call
Of storm-winds o'er the sleeted hill!

A MOMENT OF DESPONDENCY.

O fearful gift of sympathy!   O heart
Too finely strung, whose silken fibers rise
Or fall with gentlest airs that blow them!   Thou
Hast suffered undeserved tortures for
Thy fond solicitude for other souls!
Misplaced, perchance, and hence the penalty;
But who shall tell the blossom when and where
It may diffuse its fragrance that a sense
Appreciative only meet its breath?
It is *too late* when song has gushed from birds
To say no ear shall thrill with ecstacy,
Receptive of its inspiration!   So
Too late when mountain cascades float in spray
Deep hidden in primeval shade, to say
No sunbeams there disclose the iris wreath!
And so the free outpouring of the wealth
Of nature's warm, untrammelled feelings, late,
Too late for calm philosophy to save
The sorrow disappointment brings.

SONG OF A SUNBEAM.

From Heaven's empyreal fount of light,
　Along a rainbow crystal way,
Between its distant walls of night,
　I roam with my companions gay!

When stars grow dim in ether's track
　We scatter o'er the mountains blue
The midnight's shadows still and black,
　And give the east its rosy hue!

Immortal as the ruling Power
　Who taught us how to flash and shine,
We still to leaf and lowly flower
　Give luster from the lamp divine!

On forms inanimate we pour
　The radiance of beauty's wing;
And human hearts may evermore
　Inspired by our rejoicings sing!

Pursuing pity's holy dream,
  Sometimes I leave my golden band,
The desolate become my theme,—
  A prisoner's cell, a trembling hand,

A buried love, a mourner's prayer,
  Betray new life and thrill in me;
I chase the storm-king from the air,
  And still the horrors of the sea!

We form the fringes of the star,
  And glow behind the vail of night;
More swift than thought the sunbeam's car,
  Nor age nor space can check its flight!

HOME INVOCATION.

Missouri, grasp thy colors now,—
 Unfurl them to the Autumn breeze,
 While every stately sister sees
Thy bloom and wealth,—thy Press and Plow!

Invoke of Fame a clarion note
 To sound o'er mountains, streams and plains,
 From Texas' shore to Huron's chains
Where waters coldly, grandly float!

Let signs of freedom cheer the scene
 Of all industrious, noble arts,
 While every gloomy shade departs
That curtains yet our country's mein!

With welcome glad, sincere and free,
 Receive thy guests from far and near,
 And make thy pleasant regions dear,
To every heart saluting thee!

Let happy anthems loyal sung
    Columbia's faithful scions prove,
    And each discordant note remove
From elements so finely strung !

Let pure ambition give its name
    To all who seek progression's road,—
    To every mind that looks to God
For broad Missouri's growing fame !

So shall the world approvals give
    To victors of a noble race,
    And history delight to trace
Thy name enrolled for aye to live !

www.ingramcontent.com/pod-product-compliance
Lightning Source LLC
Chambersburg PA
CBHW020846270326
41928CB00006B/566